EXPLORING FATIMA

EXPLORING FATIMA

World Apostolate of Fatima

AMI Press
Washington, New Jersey

A presentation of the proceedings of the National Fatima Symposium at Marymount University, Arlington, Virginia, July 7-9, 1989.

Imprimatur: Rev. John B. Szymanski
            Vicar General
            Diocese of Metuchen

N.B. The imprimatur implies nothing more than that the material contained in this publication has been examined by diocesan censors and that nothing contrary to faith and morals has been found therein.

Cover photo
This sculpture of the angel presenting the Host and chalice to Lucia, Jacinta and Francisco at the Loca do Cabeço captures the essence of the Eucharistic element of the Fatima message.

©Copyright 1989, The Blue Army of Our Lady of Fatima, U.S.A. Inc.
All rights reserved.

Library of Congress Catalog Card Number 91-72490

ISBN 1-56036-003-8

Contents

Preface	ix
Must Catholics Believe in Fatima? The Place of Private Revelation in the Church Rev. Eamon R. Carroll, O.Carm.	1
Setting the Stage for Fatima: The World Situation in 1917 Rev. Robert I. Bradley, S.J.	14
Reflections on the Fatima Children Rev. John De Marchi, I.M.C.	24
Mary: Catechist at Fatima Rev. Frederick L. Miller	34
Sacred Scripture and the Message of Fatima Rev. René Laurentin	56
Mary's Option for the Poor Rev. Bertrand de Margerie, S.J.	94
Questions from the Audience and Responses from the Symposium Speakers' Panel Rev. Frederick L. Miller Rev. Eamon R. Carroll, O. Carm. Rev. Bertrand de Margerie, S.J. Rev. John De Marchi, I.M.C.	99

Preface

Marymount University in Arlington, Virginia was the site of our First National Fatima Symposium. Over three hundred members of the Fatima Apostolate gathered there on Friday, July 7, 1989 for a weekend symposium on the Message of Our Lady of Fatima.

Nationally and internationally renowned scholars presented fresh and refreshing insights into the significance of Fatima for our times. Rev. Eamon R. Carroll, O. Carm., noted systematic theologian and Mariologist, tackled the question: "Must Catholics believe in Fatima? The Place of Private Revalation in the Church." "Setting the Stage for Fatima; the World Situation in 1971" was the theme of Jesuit historian Rev. Robert I. Bradley. Missionary priest and Fatima authority Rev. John De Marchi, I.M.C. presented his reflections on Lucia, Jacinta and Francisco. Rev. René Laurentin, internationally renowned Scripture scholar and Mariologist, presented a master paper on "Sacred Scripture and the Message of Fatima." In place of symposium speaker Msgr. Eugene Kevane, Ph.D., who had suffered a heart attack, I personally prepared a paper titled "Mary: Catechist at Fatima." Having studied under Msgr. Kevane in graduate school, I sought to be faithful to his solid doctrine and fine insights in the field of catechesis. The French Jesuit theologian, Rev. Bertrand de Margerie, rounded out the program with his magnificent homily, "Mary's Option for the Poor."

The speakers formed a panel at the end and answered the questions of symposium participants. The texts of all these presentations, including the panel discussions, are contained in this volume. It is the hope of this apostolate that the proceedings of this symposium will draw many, especially those who are students of theology and spirituality today, into the exceedingly profound message of Our Lady of Fatima.

On May 13, 1989, His Holiness Pope John Paul II, solemnly declared that Francisco and Jacinta, the two youngest seers of Fatima, had lived lives of "heroic virtue" and are, therefore, candidates for beatification and canonization in the Catholic Church. If the message of Fatima was able to so transform two little children, there may still be hope for us, poor sinners, in an age so deeply defaced by the phenomenon of atheism and revolt against Almighty God. The texts contained in this volume suggest that the phenomenon and message of Fatima form the antidote of this revolt.

And that this humble volume might bear good fruit in the life of the Church, we ask the prayers of Sister Lucia, the surviving seer of Fatima, and dedicate the work to Our Lady, Cause of Our Joy—Our Lady of Fatima.

> Rev. Frederick L. Miller
> Shrine of the Immaculate Heart of Mary
> Washington, N.J.
> Solemnity of the Immaculate Conception, 1989

Must Catholics Believe in Fatima?

The Place of Private Revelation in the Church

Rev. Eamon R. Carroll, O. Carm.

Before I plunge into my assigned topic, permit me to state my own strong belief that Our Lady did indeed appear to the children at Fatima in 1917. I have been a pilgrim there on occasion. My Carmelite religious family built a monastery there in 1947 and in the early fifties constructed an international center for lay Carmelites—Casa Beato Nuno—named for the national hero of Portugal who ended his life as a Carmelite brother (d. 1431). I rejoice in the fact that the Mother of Jesus appeared to the children as Our Lady of Mount Carmel in the final extraordinary meeting of October 13, 1917. Father Miller graciously invited me as a theologian to offer these reflections on the "The place of Private Revelation in the Church," and to attempt to answer the compelling question, "Must Catholics Believe in Fatima?"

I have inverted the order of the title in the program, so as to consider the more general aspects first; that is, the place of private revelation in the Church, before continuing on to the questions about Fatima. The reason for taking up the more general question first is to give us sufficient context in which to examine the place of Fatima—specifically, the revelations associated with Our Lady's appearances.

Private revelations and apparitions of Our Lady go back almost to the beginning of Christianity. St. Gregory of Nyssa (d. 394) tells of an appearance of Our Lady and St. John the Apostle to St. Gregory the Wonderworker a century earlier (d. ca. 270). Our Lady spoke to St. John, asking him to make known to Gregory "the mystery of true piety." St. John replied that he would gladly do so in order to give pleasure to the Mother of Jesus. There are some extraordinary correspondences between this third century event and Our Lady's appearance at Knock, in the west of Ireland, on August 21, 1879, (which the Holy Father visited for its centenary in 1979). At Knock there was no verbal message but a group of people saw Our Lady and St. John, and also St. Joseph and the figure of a lamb on an altar.

We recall the appearance to Juan Diego in Mexico of Our lady of Guadalupe in 1531, which led to millions of conversions. In the past century-and-a-half we know of a number of famous manifestations, beginning with the appearances to St. Catherine Labouré in 1830 that led to the miraculous medal; La Salette in 1846 to two shepherd children; Lourdes above all in 1858; and also, if less known, Pontmain, France in 1871, and two in Belgium. In our century, there have been Beauraing, 1932-33, and Banneux, 1933 (Our Lady of the Poor). And, of course, there is Fatima in 1917, with the preliminary appearances of the angel in 1916 and the subsequent explanations granted Lucia in the twenties, thirties and forties.

Here are some ground rules about "private revelation." Each point will be further developed and applied to Fatima. The phrase "private revelation" is a technical term. It means revelations that are distinct from "public revelation." The words "public revelation" are also technical terminology for the revelation given to the apostles, which closed with the death of the last apostle in such a way that nothing can be added to it.

At the Second Vatican Council it was said that the full revelation of the supreme God was brought to completion in Jesus Christ (*Dei Verbum*, No. 7). What is known as "the deposit of the faith" was completed with the death of the last apostle and is enshrined as a living inheritance in the Scriptures and in the Tradition of the Church, confided to the Church for its transmission, preservation and interpretation. The council stated it:

> This tradition which comes from the Apostles develops in the Church with the help of the Holy Spirit. For there is a growth in the understanding of the realities and the words which have been handed down. This happens through the contemplation and study made by believers [we may note that believers include theologians in their prayer and research], who treasure these things in their hearts (cf. Lk 2:9, 51) through the intimate understanding of spiritual things they experience, and through the preaching of those who have received through episcopal succession the sure gift of truth [*Dei Verbum*, No. 8].

The council expanded on the teaching role of the pope and the bishops: they are to "strive painstakingly and by appropriate means to inquire properly into that revelation and to give apt expression to its contents. But they do not accept any new public revelation as part of the devine deposit of faith" (*Lumen Gentium*, No. 25). At the same time the conciliar Fathers spoke also of the prophetic office of the holy people of God, noting that the Holy Spirit distributes special graces among the faithful of every rank, "these charismatic gifts are to be received with thanksgiving and consolation, for they are exceedingly suitable and useful for the needs of the Church" (No. 12). Though extraordinary gifts are not to be rashly sought—one is reminded of the advice of St. John of the Cross (d. 1591)—Church authorities are reminded at the same time not to extinguish the Spirit, but to test all things and hold fast to that which is good (1 Thes 5, 12 and 19−21). Apparitions and private revelations can be counted among the charismatic gifts thus meant for the building up of the Church.

Some private revelations remain totally hidden and are intended only for the recipients. We have no idea how many these are, or how often they occur. They may well be fairly common, known only to the persons thus favored and to spiritual directors or confessors. Other private revelations become public and known to a wide circle of the faithful, or even, as in the case of Lourdes and Fatima, to the whole world, or for Guadalupe, throughout the Americas.

A particular or "prophetic" revelation that reaches beyond its immediate recipients is judged by the Church in terms of its correspondence to public revelation, i.e., to the Scriptures and constant traditional teaching. The first need is to establish the genuinness of the claims. There come into play the norms of critical history as well as the rules of normal and abnormal psychology. After such investigations if the results are favorable —the Church gives permission for common acts associated with the events, such as pilgrimages and special prayers at the sacred site. Approval is normally left to the local bishop. At times a pattern of veneration and public worship, in which the bishop himself takes part, amounts to the same sort of approval, as seems to have been the case at Knock in Ireland, sealed by the papal visit in 1979.

With respect to Fatima, we may note the papal visit of Paul VI in 1967, on its fiftieth anniversary, and also the publication on that occasion of one of his major Marian letters, *Signum Magnum* "the great sign," title taken from the twelfth chapter of the Apocalypse: "the great sign that appeared in the sky, the woman clothed with the sun." Pope John Paul II went to Fatima on May 12-13, 1982, in thanksgiving for deliverance from the assassination attempt just one year before. On that occasion the Holy Father renewed the entrustment of the world to the Immaculate Heart of Mary, and he asked all bishops to join him in renewing this act on the weekend of the Feast of the Annunciation in 1984, to conclude the jubilee year of Redemption. (The World Apostolate of Fatima has published an attractive pamphlet with the Holy Father's Fatima homily of May 13, 1982: *"And from that hour. . .",* opening words taken from St. John's account of Calvary.

Even with such strong signs of papal support, the Church adheres to the rules set down in the eighteenth century by Pope Benedict XIV to the effect that "assent to apparitions is of human faith, following the rules of prudence." We give divine faith to public revelation, where the Church teaches infallibly: for private revelations, as with apparitions, only human faith is involved. The recipient of the extraordinary experience may be bound in conscience by divine faith because of the immediacy of the happening, though even here as we know from St. Teresa of Jesus, the visionary must submit his or her judgment to the authority of the Church, by way of a confessor or spiritual advisor, or by way of the the bishop.

In a document from 1907, Pope St. Puis X reiterated the rules of Benedict XIV as they had also been renewed in statements from the Congregation of Rites in 1875 with respect to Lourdes and La Salette, Pius X said: "Such apparitions or revelations have neither been approved nor condemned by the Apostolic See, but it has been permitted piously to belive them merely with human faith, with due regard to the tradition they bear."

In some cases the privileged recipients of revelation have been canonized. We think of St. Margaret Mary Alacoque (d. 1690), who was God's instrument in promoting devotion to the Sacred Heart. In the sadly neglected great letter of Pius XII, *Haurietis Aquas* (1956), on the doctrine and devotion of the Sacred Heart, it is noted that what was revealed to St. Margaret Mary was nothing new in Catholic doctrine, and that under the symbol of the heart of Jesus his love is recalled. The two saints we think of in terms of the appearances of Our Lady are St. Bernadette (d. 1879) and St. Catherine Labouré (d. 1876). St. Catherine (canonized 1947) was the secret recipient of appearances of Our Lady leading to the "miraculous medal" of the Immaculate Conception. Pius XI said of her: "Hidden with Christ in God, Sister Catherine knew how to guard the secret of her Queen."

St. Bernadette Soubirous, as a girl of fourteen, was favored with eighteen appearances of Our Lady at the grotto of Massabielle by the swift-flowing Gave in 1858. She was beatified in 1925 and canonized in 1933. Lourdes has been an inexhaustible place of grace, providing healings of body and soul, ever since Our Lady's gracious visit in 1858. It has been said that the greatest proof of Lourdes was St. Bernadette. She said of herself: "The Holy Virgin made use of me. Then she put me back in my place. I am content with that and there I remain."

In the canonization of both saints, as also of St. Margaret Mary, the focus was on their heroic virtue, although popular interest was strongly stimulated by the apparitions. In the liturgical celebrations associated with these saints, and even with the Feast of Our Lady of Lourdes in our calendar for February 11, the emphasis is on the Marian mystery that is being commemorated —the Immaculate Conception—rather than on the events of the apparitions. In the current calendar, February 11 is titled simply "the Blessed Virgin Mary of Lourdes," whereas the previous title (used until 1969) was "the apparition of the Immaculate B. V. M." This reason was given for the change of title: "that it may be more clearly seen that the object of the celebration is the Blessed Virgin herself, not the historical fact of her appearance."

Appearances of Our Lady are frequent phenomena in the lives of the saints, but they are not requirements for sainthood. Some saints, well remembered for their great devotion to the Blessed Virgin, were not favored with apparitions or special revelations. Obviously, Christian sanctity does not include the requirement of apparitions. The main requirement is heroic virtue in union wtth Christ. In the cases we do know about, such apparitions favored the holiness of the recipients. A short list would include such names as St. Dominic, St. Ignatius Loyola, and the Carmelites St. Teresa of Jesus, St. Mary Magdalen de Pazzi, and St. Thérèse of the Child Jesus.

In their enormous variety the saints serve the church as summaries of Catholic doctrine. This is one reason the Church is so careful—even ultra-cautious—about claims of private revelation and apparitions. At the time of the appearances to Bernadette, between February 11 and July 16, fifty false visionaries were reported. As the second preface for the saints from the Missal has it, holy men and holy women are living witnesses of God's unchanging love. We are called to imitate them, for "they inspire us by their heroic lives." We count on their intercession, for "they help us by their constant prayers," and assist us also to be living signs of God's saving power. All their holy activity is at the service of the Church, for through these holy people God renews the Church in every age.

All three elements are verified in authentic apparitions: example, intercession and the ecclesial service of the saints. The seer who lives in accordance with the message of the revelation emphasizes in actual life neglected aspects of Christian commitment: prayer, penance, the Sacraments, charity. In the saints who have been beatified and canonized we find four qualities in the apparitions to them of Our Lady: first, their experience is in complete accord with the Gospels; second, it is at the service of the Church; third, the apparition has witness value; finally, there is centrality of charity, so abundantly documented in the lives of St. Catherine, St. Bernadette, and St. Thérèse.

Additional light on the place of private revelation in the life of the Church can be found in the liturgy. We have noted how guardedly the Church incorporates revelations and apparitions into liturgical celebrations, not imposing on believers the initial events that gave rise to popular pilgrimages, to special prayers, even to commemorative Masses. For the votive Masses of Our Lady at Marian shrines, and in the universal calendar of the Church (the single example of Our Lady of Lourdes, February 11), the devotion is to the person of the Blessed Virgin, whatever the occasion that led to the choice of date or place.

For the liturgies associated with apparitions and their attendant revelations three factors enter in: The first is approval by Church authorities, in the first place the local bishop. Above all, the Marian mystery commemorated must be part of the Church's teaching. In the appearances to St. Catherine Labouré, the Immaculate Conception was already a common belief; by the time of Lourdes (in 1858) the Church had solemnly defined Our Lady's freedom from original sin as a dogma of the faith. When the Holy Father gives his approval to the feast, the liturgies involved can be regarded as practically immune from error. In assessing the bond between the liturgy and apparitions, a second factor is the degree of the Church's proposal and acceptance. The resurrection of Jesus is a dogma of the faith. Our Lady's Assumption was generally accepted before 1950, as it has been for many centuries, but only with its definition on November 1, 1950 did it become a matter of divine and Catholic faith, clearly belonging to public revelation. The Presentation of Mary on November 21, an ancient Easter feast, is regarded by the Church as a pious legend, although its deeper meaning of Mary's holiness and lifelong dedication to God is a matter of faith. A third factor in liturgical commemoration of apparitions is that the liturgy reflects a true development of doctrine in the Church. This was true of the long and slow history of the Immaculate Conception. "Praying shapes believing" is an ancient axiom of Christian experience.

MUST CATHOLICS BELIEVE IN FATIMA?

Now to the question; "Must Catholics Believe in Fatima?" What has been said so far can help us formulate a carefully nuanced answer to that question, because a simple "yes" or "no" is neither a sufficient nor a fair reply. We consider in order the reaction of Church authorities, prayers associated with Fatima both in liturgy and devotions, and finally, the message of Fatima. I have not proposed the holiness of the seers, not out of any doubt concerning their holiness, but because Lucia is still alive, and the causes of Francisco and Jacinta have just begun (they were declared "venerable" on May 13, 1989), with the result that it would be premature to comment on this aspect here.

How have Church authorities reacted to Fatima? Initially, the local pastor was far from convinced by the reports of the children, though he had the wisdom to write down carefully his conversations with them. The local bishop and then the Cardinal of Lisbon soon set up a board of inquiry to take testimony from all concerned. The canonical inquiry led to the decision of May 13, 1930, that the claims were worthy of human faith. Official devotion to Our Lady of the Rosary of Fatima was approved. By then, Portuguese pilgrims had come in ever-increasing numbers, and the fame of Fatima had gone beyond the borders of Portugal. Bishop da Silva began the construction of a basilica on the site. The bishops issued a joint pastoral on May 12, 1942. A million pilgrims came on October 13, 1942, Pope Pius XII took the occasion to send a radio message in which he consecrated the world to the Immaculate Heart of Mary, with a veiled reference to Russia. He renewed that consecration in Rome during the Feast of the Immaculate Conception on December 8, 1942, and he chose to close the Holy Year at Fatima on October 13, 1951, sending Cardinal Tedeschini as his legate. He renewed the consecration, and again addressed by radio the million people there assembled.

Pope Paul VI went to Fatima in 1967. Pope John Paul II was there in 1982 and in his homily of May 13 he said, "If the Church has accepted the message of Fatima, it is above all because that message contains a truth and a call whose basic content is the truth and the call of the Gospel itself." A tireless pilgrim to Marian shrines in every one of the many countries he visits, the Holy Father has written and spoken inspiringly of the presence of Mary at these privileged places where we:

> seek to meet the Mother of the Lord, the one who is blessed because she believed, first among believers and therefore the Mother of Emmanuel (God-with-us). This is the message of centers like Guadalupe, Lourdes, Fatima. Among them how could I fail to mention the one in my own native land, Jasna Gora [Czestochowa]? One could

perhaps speak of a specific (geography) of faith and Marian devotion [who with better right than the great traveler Pope John Paul II], which includes all these special places of pilgrimage where the People of God seek to meet the Mother of God in order to find, within the radius of the maternal presence of her (who believed) a strengthening of their own faith. (*Redemptoris Mater, No. 28.*)

In the general calendar of the Church three of Our Lady's days are associated with sacred places, each commemorating a blessed presence of the Mother of Jesus. The first is Our Lady of Lourdes, the second comes from the homeland of Jesus and his Mother, Our Lady of Mount Carmel, and the third is the dedication of the basilica of St. Mary Major, the principal Roman Church in her honor.

With respect to prayers associated with Fatima, the local liturgy does not specifically mention the apparitions. We have seen that even for Lourdes the current liturgy is silent about the apparitions to St. Bernadette, but the main ingredients of the Fatima message—prayer, penance, reparation, the Immaculate Heart of Mary—are woven into the approved prayers, as in the prayer said after the decades of the Rosary: "Oh my Jesus save us from our sins, deliver us from the fires of hell. Lead all souls into heaven, especially those who have most need of your mercy."

There is no doubt that Fatima has greatly encouraged devotion to the Immaculate Heart of Mary, from the initial six appearances of 1917 through subsequent revelations that Lucia has told us about. It may be said that the theme of the Immaculate Heart, with its constellation of associated doctrines, is the most original and most specific element of the Fatima message. When the Sacred Congregation of Rites approved the new Mass of the Feast of the Immaculate Heart of Mary in 1945 and extended it to the entire Church (kept on the Saturday after the Second Sunday after Pentecost), it gave this explanation: "Under the symbol of the Heart of the Mother of God, her eminent holiness and especially her most ardent love for God and her Son Jesus are venerated with piety, as well as her maternal devotion to men ransomed by the divine blood.

When Pope John Paul II was at Fatima in 1982 he renewed the dedication to Our Lady that his predecessors had made. It is worth noting that in the strict sense "consecration" is an act of religion that can be properly made only to God Himself. This clarification was made most carefully by the Holy Father at Fatima and subsequent explanations, especially on March 24−25, 1984, when he asked all the bishops of the world to make a formula which he called "an act of entrusting" to Our Lady and her Immaculate Heart. The core consecration is a consecration to God, as Jesus consecrated Himself at the Last Supper. The Mother of Jesus is the perfect exemplar of total consecration to God.

The formula of entrusting the world to the Blessed Virgin for the Annunciation of 1984, read:

> "Behold, as we stand before you, Mother of Christ, before your Immaculate Heart, we desire, together with the whole Church, to unite ourselves with the consecration which, for love of us, your Son made of Himself to the Father. "For their sake," He said, "I consecrate myself that they also may be consecrated in the truth" (Jn 17:19). We wish to unite ourselves with our Redeemer in this his consecration for the world and for the human race, which in his divine heart has the power to obtain pardon and to secure reparation.

Again we ask; "Must Catholics believe in Fatima?" The answer is two fold. So far as the heart of the Fatima message goes—prayer, penance, reparation and the compassionate Immaculate Heart of Mary—the Church's approval is absolute. No Catholic is free to reject these key aspects of Christian belief and practice. The Church's judgment here is infallible because these are matters that affect the very core of our Christian and Catholic lives. As far as the particular circumstances that gave rise to the Fatima message are concerned the Church has warmly recommended acceptance of the apparitions, but only as a matter of human faith, so that a Catholic is not obliged to accept the initial accounts of 1917, the appearances of the angel in 1916, and subsequent revelations communicated to Lucia. This may seem strange, but we cannot make obligations where the Church does not command us. It is important that we not impose on others the obligation to accept private revelations. Very instructive in this regard is the advice of Pope Paul VI in his greatest Marian letter (February 2, 1974, *Marialis Cultus,* on the promotion of devotion to Mary). The letter explains the strong place of Our Lady in the revised liturgy. It has a section on the Rosary and the Angelus. (We recall the role of the Rosary at Lourdes, La Salette and Fatima.) At the end of his warm pages about the Rosary, Pope Paul wrote:

> In concluding these observations, which give proof of the concern and esteem which the Apostolic See has for the Rosary of the Blessed Virgin, we desire at the same time that this very worthy devotion should not be propagated in a way that is too one-sided or exclusive. The Rosary is an excellent prayer, but the faithful should feel serenely free in its regard. They should be drawn to its calm recitation by its intrinsic appeal (No. 55). This is surely applicable to Fatima and to other apparitions, for they must not be used to restrict the legitimate freedom of loyal sons and daughters of the Church.

The advice of the bishops of the United States is similar. Their joint pastoral, *Behold Your Mother: Woman of Faith* (November 21, 1973) states:

> These providential happenings serve as reminders to us of basic Christian themes: prayer, penance, and the necessity of the sacraments. After due investigation, the Church has approved the pilgrimages and other devotions associated

with certain private revelations. She has also at times certified the holiness of their recipients by beatification and canonization, for example, St. Bernadette of Lourdes and St. Catherine Labouré. The Church judges the devotions that have sprung from these extraordinary events in terms of its own traditional standards. Catholics are encouraged to practice such devotions when they are in conformity with authentic devotion to Mary. Even when a "private revelation" has spread to the entire world, as in the case of Our Lady of Lourdes, and has been recognized in the liturgical calendar, the Church does not make mandatory the acceptance either of the original story or of particular forms of piety springing from it. With the Vatican Council we remind true lovers of Our Lady of the danger of superficial sentiment and vain credulity. Our faith does not seek new gospels, but leads us to a filial love toward our Mother and to the imitation of her virtues (No. 100, and in the conciliar constitution on the Church, No. 67).

A FINAL WORD

For a personal closing testimony: I am a son of Our Lady of Mount Carmel. It has been my privilege since 1949 to study the theology of the Blessed Virgin Mary, Holy Mother of God and our most loving spiritual mother. I regard her appearances as privileged illustrations of divine condescension, as private manifestations for the public good of God's designs at precise historical moments. I see Fatima as a sign in our time of God's merciful concerns for us, a loving lesson offered by the Mother of Jesus (now in glory with her Risen Son) of our final destiny and our present dignity, reminding us of prayer and penance, and promising us peace and joy through our union with Christ now and forever.

Setting the Stage for Fatima: The World Situation in 1917

Rev. Robert I. Bradley, S.J.

The topic assigned me in this symposium is meant to fulfill the injunction given us a quarter of a century ago by the Second Vatican Council, when reminded of our responsibility to read "the signs of the times" (cf. *Gaudium et Spes*, No. 4). As we now know, by the authority of the Ordinary Magisterium of the Church and by the experience of nearly three quarters of a century, what happened at Fatima in the six-month period from spring through autumn in 1917 was a "sign of the times"— a sign for this entire century, a sign of near-Biblical reality (cf. *Apoc* 12) from heaven itself.

Let us examine the date 1917. What can we see in that year itself as a "sign"? Well, for one attuned to the rhythms of history, that year could have been predicted as a momentous one. Consider what happened exactly four hundred years earlier, in 1517. That year marked the birth of Protestantism. All Protestants regard the incident of Luther's theses at Wittenberg as the great overture to the Reformation. Exactly two hundred years later, the year 1717 marked the birth of Freemasonry with the establishment of the first formal Masonic lodge in England. There is a connection between these two events, separated as they are by two centuries. In the sixteenth century occurred the great revolt against the Catholic Church. In the eighteenth century that revolt deepened and widened into a revolt against Christianity as such. After another two centuries, in 1917 the third stage is reached. The year 1917 marks the birth of Atheism through the establishment of the first officially atheist regime in history. Here is the real "dialectic" of Marxist ideology now triumphant in Russia. The unravelling of the Creed from its end to its beginning from the Third Article through the Second Article to the First Article. The world has "progressed" from the rejection of the Church to the rejection of Christ and ultimately to the rejection of God Himself. What a "fearful symmetry" this "Modern History" has! What can be the end from such beginnings!

Let us look at the year 1917 in sharper focus. Consider its context now, not in centuries but in decades. What was the second decade of the twentieth century like? As we know, world history was dominated then by a single "world" event: the "Great War" of 1914-1918. (That was indeed its proper name, given it by the British. Already in 1914 it was called the "World War".) Nothing like it had happened before and nothing like it could possibly happen again. Wasn't it "the war to *end* all wars"?

Later it was renamed "World War I" owing to the *Second World War*, which broke out in 1939 (not to mention "World War III" which for nearly forty years we have been dreading). World War II was in almost every way a greater war than World War I—in duration, in geographical spread, in numbers of combatants and nations involved, in violence, in destruction. Yet World War I remains the "Great War," for it marked the great change in world history. All the subsequent wars are but play outs of that change. Luther's revolt was certainly outclassed by Calvin's in the sixteenth century, just as in the eighteenth century the original Masonic lodge in England was outclassed by the Grand Orient Lodge in France. In the twentieth century, World War I was in similar fashion outclassed by World War II. Nevertheless, the *real* revolution occurred in World War I: the revolution against God in its first formal and fundamental phase, i.e., the utter secularization of the world powers.

No sooner had World War I begun in 1914 than this exact diagnosis was clearly and formally made. On November first of that year, after it had become evident that the anticipated quick revolution of the war had been frustrated by the battles of Marne (on the Western Front) and Tannenberg (on the Eastern Front), Benedict XV, the newly elected successor to Pius X (who had died amid "the guns of August"), issued his inaugural encyclical, entitled *Ad Beatissimi Apostolorum*. The new pope was a jurist by training, and with a lawyer's precision he outlined four causes of this new and terrible war:

1. lack of mutual love among men,
2. disregard for authority,
3. unjust quarrels between the various classes and
4. a material prosperity had become the absorbing object of human endeavor, as though there were nothing higher and better to be named.

Surely, there is no better diagnosis for World War I than this. The Holy Father, both by the charism of his office and by the natural talent that he brought to that office as a man of vision and a student of history, listed four causes. Notice the linkage and the sequence: When *charity*, the greatest virtue of all, goes, *obedience* must soon follow, for obedience to authority is inevitably undermined; that is the signal for *justice* to disappear, i.e., justice as the basic sense of fairness, of honesty. Finally, when justice goes, the last thing left—the basic *sanity* of rational nature—is imperiled and succumbs. For it is irrationality, it is madness to see man's destiny as something limited to this world, as though this world could ever satisfy the human heart.

The Holy Father pleaded for peace. If these are the causes of war, then what we must do is go back and reverse those steps, as it were. We must regain *rationality, justice, obedience and love*; if we do so, then this horror will be lifted from us.

As we know, and as Pope Benedict himself knew soon enough, his words were not heeded. They were lost amid the din of war—

the speeches of the politicians and the guns at the front. And so the World War went on. What already struck the world as an immeasurable catastrophe—that world of 1914—only became *worse*. The year 1915 brought a numbness to the initial shock, and then 1916 brought unspeakable tragedy. At Verdun and the Somme, the slaughter of over a million and a half soldiers staggered the world, yet the war went on.

In 1917, two more names registered the horror on the Western Front: the Chemin des Dames for the French and Passchendaele for the British. I came across one attempt to describe this horror in a little book by Dr. Warren Carroll. Entitled simply *1917,* it is an excellent study. Dr. Carroll quotes a war correspondent who unwittingly sets the stage for Fatima:

> No pen or drawing can convey this country—the normal setting of the battles taking place day and night, month after month. Evil and the incarnate fiend alone can be master of this war, and no glimmer of God's hand is seen anywhere. Sunset and sunrise are blasphemous; they are mockeries to man; only the black rain out of the bruised and swollen clouds all through the entire black of night is fit atmosphere in such a land. The rain drives on, the stinking mud becomes evilly yellow, the shell-holes fill up with green-white water, the roads and tracks are covered in inches of slime, the black dying trees ooze and sweat and the shells never cease. They alone plunge overhead, tearing away the rotting tree stumps...annihilating, maiming, maddening, they plunge into the grave which is this land; one huge grave, and cast upon it the poor dead. It is unspeakable, godless, hopeless.

This is indeed the setting of the stage. And it is real, not something conjured up by the vision of the apocalyptic writer, but the report of a journalist of what it was like in the heart of Western civilization after three years of unimaginable war.

In August 1917, after taking infinite pains to follow all the proper procedures set down in civilized discourse in terms of diplomatic contacts, Benedict XV proposed a peace plan to the belligerents. This papal peace proposal was carried to Berlin by a newly consecrated archbishop named Eugenio Pacelli, while other Vatican officials contacted the other capitals. (Pacelli was consecrated to the episcopacy in the Sistine Chapel on May 13, 1917—a date to remember.) The Holy Father's plan consisted of seven points:

1. the moral force of right to replace the material force of arms

2. simultaneous and reciprocal reduction of armaments

3. international arbitration

4. freedom and community of the seas

5. reciprocal renunciation of war indemnities

6. evacuation and restoration of all occupied territories

7. examination, in a conciliatory spirit, of all territorial claims.

These seven points can be construed as rather obvious. In fact, these seven points were amplified the following year by the American president, Woodrow Wilson, into fourteen points. So what is so extraordinary about this papal plan?

What is extraordinary (aside from the fact that this was the first serious peace proposal since the beginning of hostilities) is that the Holy Father is meeting the world on its own terms. As the representative of the oldest sovereignty in Europe, he pleaded with his fellow sovereigns in both camps to recognize the sanity of this settlement. *Justice* was also invoked, but in his realism he left it there. Perhaps on those terms alone the war-weary and humbled Powers will come to their senses. Later, perhaps, he could address them on the issues of obedience and love.

Meanwhile, the Holy Father did have another peace plan, one which he did not send to the high and mighty of this world, but instead to those who could do something about the situation of this world. He appealed through *prayer* to the faithful people of the Church. As early as 1915, Benedict XV made this prayer:

> In this hour made terrible with burning hate, with bloodshed and with slaughter, once more may Thy divine Heart be moved to pity. Pity the countless mothers in anguish for the fate of their sons; pity the numberless families now bereaved of their fathers; pity Europe over which broods such havoc and disaster. Do Thou inspire rulers and peoples with counsels of meekness, do Thou heal the discords that tear the nations asunder; Thou Who didst shed Thy Precious Blood that they might live as brothers, bring men together once more in loving harmony. And as once before to the cry of the Apostle Peter: "Save us, Lord, we perish!" Thou didst answer with words of mercy and didst still the raging waves, so now deign to hear our trustful prayer, and give back to the world peace and tranquility.
>
> And do thou, O most holy Virgin, as in other times of sore distress, be now our help, our protection and our safeguard.

That was the prayer of the Holy Father which in his humility he made public, at Eastertime in 1915. But he wanted to add to his own prayers the prayer of others. The Vicar of Christ turned to the littlest members of his flock, the children. These are the words he spoke a few months later, in July 1916, to an audience of children in the Vatican:

> In order that the record of this moment may remain graven on your minds all your lives, and that you may ever have to remember what you heard at this fatal time from the very lips of Christ's Vicar, learn from us, my children,

how for two long years men who were once innocent and affectionate like you, and are so no longer, have been tearing and killing each other. ...You are taking part in the most fearful expiation that God, in his hidden and infinite design, ever wrought by the hands of guilty society. ...Therefore we have resolved to betake ourself, as to a last plank in shipwreck, to invoking the help of God through the all-powerful means of your innocence. ...Stretch out a hand then, dear and all-powerful childern, to the Vicar of Christ and strengthen his unceasing desires with your precious prayers. Will your parents, your brothers, all the older members of your families follow in your humble footsteps?...You know what We desire. We desire that mankind may cease from hatred and slaughter, and after having been so wickedly fellows of Cain may become instead fellows of Abel by the works of grace, labor and pardon. ...May God, who spared from death the sons of the Hebrews through the blood which gleamed red as a sign on the doors of their houses, spare you and your household and the entire world every further shedding of blood by the merits of that infinitely precious stream which bathed the cross of the Divine Son and which today, after the mystic banquet, gleams red on your lips, symbol once again of the Redemption and the pardon which Jesus alone can give.

It is pathetic, is it not, to hear the Holy Father thus pleading with these little ones to help him bring about the return of peace to the world?

Following this address, in May 1917 he wrote to one of his Cardinals:

Our earnestly pleading voice, invoking the end of the vast conflict, the suicide of civilized Europe, was then and has remained ever since unheard. Indeed, it seemed that the dark tide of hatred grew higher and wider among the belligerent nations and drew other countries into its frightful sweep, multiplying ruin and massacre. Nevertheless our confidence was not lessened. Since all graces which the Author of all good designs to grant to the poor children of Adam, by a loving design of his Divine Providence, are dispensed through the hands of the most holy Virgin, we wish that the petition of her most afflicted children, more than ever in this terrible hour, may turn with lively confidence to the august Mother of God.

The task assigned me in this symposium is now fulfilled; we have before us the setting of the stage for Fatima. This last message of Benedict XV is the immediate context of Fatima, for it was written just one week before the first apparition of Our Lady in May 1917. The time was complete; Our Lady had heard his prayer.

Yet, our story is not complete. In a sense, it has only begun! For "the setting of the stage for Fatima" includes not only the events that *preceded* it but the events that *accompanied* it as well. Let me conclude with a review of the two great events that accompanied Fatima in that fateful year of 1917 and that became inextricably bound with the history of the entire century. They were Russia's exit from the war and America's entrance into it. Let us look briefly at each event in turn.

By 1917 the once mighty Russian Empire was reeling in defeat at the hands of the German armies. The rule of the Czar was all but fiction and the country was verging on anarchy. Then in March 1917 came revolution. This was not the revolution that has been celebrated since in Moscow's Red Square, i.e., the "October Revolution" of 1917. (Actually, by our reckoning, it occurred in November. Russia's calendar at the time was not the Gregorian but the Julian.) There were *two* successive revolutions in Russia in 1917. In March the Empire was overthrown and a provisional government was set up. This government, under Alexander Kerensky, attempted to maintain order at home and discipline in the army at the front, while calling for a constitutional convention to establish a new definitive regime. As we all know, the provisional government's failure was complete. For a full half year—from spring through autumn—Russia was in utter chaos. The fighting front had disintegrated and the deserting soldiers came home to anarchy. At this point there emerged the man who would lead the *second* revolution, first in Russia and then in the world at large: Vladimir Ilich Ulyanov, alias Lenin. Suffice it to say that within ten days, by the middle of November 1917, his plan regarding Russia had been realized. Lenin had liquidated the provisional government and replaced it with the dictatorship of the proletariat, under the supreme government of the Soviets.

Meanwhile, the United States of America had gone to war, with the declaration of war in April 1917. By autumn of 1917 the first American troops arrived on the Western Front. President Wilson's initial intention, when he asked congress for a declaration of war, was to achieve "peace without victory." What he envisioned was a conciliatory act. By going to war he hoped to bring the Germans to their senses, to make them see the futility of their desperate offensive at the time. American intervention was to bring equilibrium to the combat, which would then lead naturally to a negotiated peace.

This aim did not last very long. It was just a matter of months before this official American policy was dismissed as unrealistic. What was aimed at now was "victory at any cost." It was going to be a war to the finish—ending not in a negotiated, but in a dictated peace. The new objective of total war and total victory was justified by the plea that we would never negotiate with the existing German and Austrian governments. This decision was, as we eventually learned, a tragedy compounded. For it meant the continuation of the war for another year and a half—with its further untold destruction and bitterness that lead to the pseudo-peace of Versailles. It is true that Woodrow Wilson tried to be a conciliatory force at the peace talks. But the tone injected into the war in the course of 1917—largely due to American intervention—had foredoomed the peace.

A parallel emerges in these two concurrent events: Russia's two-staged revolution and America's two-staged involvement in the war. In each event we see an irreversible move toward *absolutism:* an absolute tyranny in Russia and an absolute impasse in the West.

These two events took place, precisely within the same six-month period (from spring to autumn of 1917), when Our Lady visited Fatima. You may ask, was not this six-month period an eventual *disaster* for the earth? How can we not say that Our Lady had delayed her answer to the Holy Father's and his children's prayers? Would not this fatal delay only create greater cynicism, seeing how vain is the intervention of heaven—seeing how this poor world of ours must somehow go it alone?

No, there is a firm but merciful logic in this "setting of the stage for Fatima." It is only when the situation is *totally hopeless* from a human viewpoint that we can truly see "the signs of the times." It is only when *total confidence* is demanded—and given—that Our Lady's coming to this world *can* be efficacious. Thus, it was not in 1914 or 1915 or 1916 or even in the first part of 1917 that she appeared. It was only by October of that year that the "miracle of the sun"—the crowning "sign" of Fatima—could be seen for what it was. Only then, with the grim realization of insanity facing the world, could *rationality* return—with *justice* following, and then *obedience*, and then *love*.

Now, seventy years later, this return is far from realized. Yet what we also know—by the sureness of that great "sign of the times" which is Fatima—is that God, through his Mother, is our one all-encompassing hope.

Reflections on the Fatima Children

Rev. John De Marchi, I.M.C.

First Beginning

The first time I went to Fatima was in June 1943. The Second World War was in full swing. I was sent to Portugal from Italy at the request of the Archbishop of Lourence Marques (Capital city of the Portuguese colony of Mozambique), who petitioned our Mission Society to open a seminary in Portugal to recruit local vocations, since all Consolata missionaries working in Mozambique were Italians.

Without any difficulty, the Bishop of Leiria authorized us to open a seminary in Fatima, provided we would give spiritual assistance to pilgrims coming to the shrine from countries outside Portugal. At that time there were only three priests in Fatima, and I was the only foreigner who could give assistance to the non-Portuguese pilgrims coming to the shrine. We were the first religious priests to set up a seminary in Fatima. Such a privilege gave me the unique opportunity of getting in touch with the families of Lucia, Jacinta and Francisco, as with the people of the area, since Fatima was still a very small village.

I had the great opportunity and privilege of living for years close to the spot where the apparitions took place. I came to know the environment, the customs and the characteristics of the people and I gained a firsthand account of the happenings during the memorable six months from May to October 1917, from those who knew them well and from those who were eyewitnesses of those extraordinary events.

THE THREE CHILDREN

My best resources were the parents of Jacinta and Francisco, Ti' Marto and Ti' Olympia, their brother John, and the family of Lucia, particularly her oldest sister Maria Rosa, who had become a sort of second mother to Lucia. These people helped to acquaint me with those precious moments and circumstances following the apparitions of Our Lady to the three youngsters.

Ti' Marto and Ti' Olympia met with me often in their home and at our seminary. I often asked Ti' Marto what kind of children Francisco and Jacinta were.

He explained that Francisco was a strong, healthy boy, very affectionate, peaceful and tranquil in temperament. Like all children he loved jokes and fun, and if he was denied his right while playing games with others, he gave in without much ado and did not seem to care if his things were taken away from him. Francisco loved music and would pass hours at a time with his reed pipe, accompanied often by Lucia or Jacinta who would sing and dance, and had a soul particularly open to the beauties spread out by the Creator around him on the Serra.

"And how was Jacinta?" I asked the mother. "Well, Jacinta, her eyes were light in color and brighter than mine. She liked to have her hair tidy and I used to do it for her every day. She always had a little jacket and a cotton shirt and shoes, for I was able to keep my children clothed. Jacinta possessed a remarkable sensitive soul. . . . When she was only five years old, she would melt with tears on hearing the story of the Passion of Our Lord. 'Poor Jesus,' she would say, 'I must never sin and make Him suffer more.' Jacinta loved to be with Lucia above all things and a day spent away from her was a day lost."

"She was always a sweet little girl," said Ti' Marto. "She particularly loved her sheep and had a special name for each one—Dove, Star, Beauty, Snow. She used to sit with them on her lap, kissing and hugging them." Dancing was also one of Jacinta's passions. "We loved dancing," says Lucia, "and any instrument we heard being played by other shepherds was enough to set us off. Jacinta, although so small, had a special talent for it."

And what about prayer?

Lucia says,

> We were told we must say the Rosary after lunch on the Serra, but as the whole day seemed too short for our play we thought of a good way of getting it done quickly. We just said "Hail Mary" on each bead and then at the end of the decade, "Our Father" with a long pause. In that way, in a few minutes the Rosary was off our minds.

So here are our three children on the eve of the great event, with their good qualities and their defects. Our Lady chose them to give her message to the world. She could have chosen others, but preferred to gaze on these innocent, simple, non-educated children and make them the heralds of her message.

THE APPARITIONS

All of us are familiar with the messages and the requests of the angel in his three apparitions and with the messages and the requests of Our Lady in her six apparitions from May 13 to October 13.

When the angel appeared to the children the first time, he told the children, "Do not be afraid. I am the Angel of Peace.

Pray with me." "My God, I believe, I adore, I hope, and I love You. I ask forgiveness for those who do not believe, nor adore, nor hope, nor love You. Pray in this way. The Hearts of Jesus and Mary are ready to listen to you."

And again when the angelic messenger appeared for the second time, he told them, "Pray! Pray! The Hearts of Jesus and Mary have merciful designs for you. Offer your prayers and sacrifices to the Most High."

"How are we to sacrifice?" asked Lucia.

"In every way you can offer a sacrifice to the Lord, in reparation for the sins by which He is offended and in supplication for sinners. Thus you will bring peace to our country. I am its guardian angel, the Angel of Portugal. Above all accept and bear with patience the sufferings which the Lord will send you."

And then he appeared for the third time, holding in his hand a chalice and above it a Host, from which a few drops of blood flowed into the chalice. Leaving the chalice and the Host suspended in the air, he prostrated himself on the ground and repeated three times the prayer:

"Most Holy Trinity, Father, Son and Holy Ghost, I adore You profoundly and I offer You the Most Precious Body, Blood, Soul and Divinity of Jesus Christ, present in all the tabernacles of the world, in reparation for the outrages, sacrileges and indifference by which He is offended. And by the infinite merits of his Most Sacred Heart and through the Immaculate Heart of Mary, I beg the conversion of poor sinners."

Afterwards, Lucia tells us, "he rose and took again the chalice and the Host and gave the Host to me and the contents of the chalice to Jacinta and Francisco to drink, saying at the same time: 'Take and drink the Body and Blood of Jesus Christ, horribly outraged by ungrateful men. Repair their crimes and console your God.' "

In the apparitions of Our Lady from May 13 to October 13, there is a constant request for prayer and sacrifice. In the first apparition Our Lady asked the children, "Will you offer yourselves to God, and bear all the sufferings which He sends you, in reparation for the sins which offend Him, and in supplication for the conversion of sinners?"

Lucia spoke for them all: "Yes, we will," she said, in a decided voice.

"Then you will have much to suffer, but the grace of God will be your strength."

The same request was repeated to the children in the following apparition on July 13:

> I want you to come back here on the thirteenth of next month. Continue to say the Rosary every day in honor of Our Lady of the Rosary, to obtain the peace of the world and the end of the war, because only she can obtain it.... Make sacrifices for sinners and say often, especially when you make a sacrifice, 'O Jesus, this is for love of Thee, for the conversion of sinners and in reparation for sins against the Immaculate Heart of Mary.'

As she said these words (continues Lucia) she opened her hands again as in the preceding months.

> The reflection which they gave out seemed to penetrate the earth and we saw a sea of fire and, plunged in this fire, devils and souls like transparent embers, black or bronzed, in human form, which floated in the fire and were carried by the flames which they themselves gave forth, together with clouds of smoke, falling on all sides—as the sparks fall in great fires—without weight or equilibrium, amidst cries of pain and despair which horrified us and made us tremble with fear. The devils could be distinguished by their horrible and terrifying forms of strange unknown animals but transparent like burning coal.

At this moment (says Ti' Marto), Lucia took a deep breath, became pale as one close to death, and was heard to cry out in terror to Our Lady, calling her by name.

Our Lady said, "You have seen hell where the souls of sinners go. To save them God wishes to establish in the world devotion to my Immaculate Heart. If you do what I tell you many souls will be saved and there will be peace. The war will end, but if men do not cease to offend God another worse one will begin. When you see a night lit by a strange unknown light, you will know that it is the sign that God gives you that he is going to punish the world for its crimes by means of war, hunger and the persecution of the Church and the Holy Father. To prevent it I shall come to ask for the consecration of Russia to my Immaculate Heart and the reparatory Communion of the First Saturdays. If my desires are fulfilled, Russia will be converted and there will be peace; if not, she will spread her errors throughout the world, causing wars and persecutions of the Church. The good will be martyred and the Holy Father will have much to suffer; various nations will be annihilated. But in the end my Immaculate Heart will triumph."

Sadly the Lady added, "Pray, pray very much and make sacrifices for sinners, for many souls go to hell because no one makes sacrifices for them."

THE CHILDREN AND THE MESSAGE

After the apparitions the lives of the children changed entirely, their lifestyles became unthinkable for children of their age and background. How can we imagine children, used to a normal life, spending long hours in prayer, practicing sacrifices and fasting in ways unthinkable even to adults?

"Many times," remarked Ti' Marto, "I found Jacinta and Francisco in a corner of the house praying and praying.... They were not doing this because we told them. We didn't teach them to spend hours in prayer, even less did we teach them to fast. Our approach was very simple: going to Mass on Sunday, saying a few prayers in the morning and at night, and that is all. The influence of the parish priest was not very encouraging. This was definitely the impact created by the apparitions of the guardian angel and of Our Lady."

"Pray! Pray! The hearts of Jesus and Mary have merciful designs for you. Offer your prayers and sacrifices to the Most High.... Accept and bear with patience the sufferings which the Lord will send you." These requests of the angel became deeply engraved on their hearts.

Lucia explained how this was so: "These words were like a light that made us understand who God is, how He loves us and wishes to be loved, the value of sacrifice and how pleasing it is to Him and how it can convert sinners. So from that moment we began to offer to God everything that mortified us, passing hours on end prostrated on the ground repeating the prayer that the angel had taught us."

We are familiar with the messages given to the children during the three apparitions of the angel and during the six apparitions of Our Lady. What impressed the children most was the request of Our Lady for prayer and penance. And we know how deeply these requests were engraved in their hearts, entirely transforming their lives. Each child's life became a life of *prayer and penance*. It is unthinkable for such young childen, ten, eight and seven, to live that kind of asceticism. It is Lucia who, in her memoirs, tells us of an episode about Francisco.

The children were pasturing their flocks. In order to prevent the flocks from eating certain fresh crops, the children split up, the girls to one side and Francisco to the other side, choosing the fringe of the wood. Lucia, who was always watchful of the younger one, told Jacinta at a certain moment to go and see if her brother was all right since he had been alone for such a long time. Jacinta called several times, but there was no reply from Francisco, and finally, worried as to his whereabouts, she hurried back to her cousin and told her that she thought her brother was lost. Lucia immediately went in search of Francisco and found him prostrated on the ground behind a stone wall. Approaching him, she touched his shoulder, shook him and said in a loud voice, "What are you doing?" Francisco replied,

I began to say the prayer of the angel and then—I started thinking—I was thinking of God Who is so sad because of all the sins, if only I could comfort Him."

In the practice of mortification they almost emulated the legendary feats of the fathers of the desert. They wanted to convert many, if not all, sinners, and they labored to excogitate new ways by which this might be accomplished by means of every conceivable suffering. Nobody outside their own intimate circle knew of or even suspected the continued prayer, the hard and uninterrupted penance. If Sister Lucia had not in part shared this we would never have known to what heroic lengths these children went.

"Why did you not speak of Our Lady's desire for sacrifice for the conversion of sinners?" Lucia was to be asked later.

"Because we were afraid they would ask us what sacrifices we did."

Lucia's manuscripts relate few of these sacrifices. Nearly all refer to Jacinta and they are sufficient to reveal to us these little giants of Christian sanctity. I will cite a few examples from Sister Lucia's account.

Thirst is one of the worst torments during the hot summer in the serra. It was one of their favorite penances; they passed nine days, and on one occasion a month, without drinking, and this in the month of August.

One day, returning from the Cova da Iria, they passed the Carreira Pond, a dirty pool of water where the women washed clothes and the animals were brought to drink. Jacinta said to Lucia, "My head aches so, and I am so thirsty. I think I will drink a little of this water."

"No, Jacinta, not from there. My mother doesn't want us to drink that water because it's dirty and might make us ill. Let's go and get some from Aunt Maria."

"No, I don't want to drink that good water. I'd like to drink this so that instead of offering Our Lady thirst I can offer this dirty water."

One day, Lucia found a piece of cord on the serra. Playing

with it she knotted it around her arm and immediately realized how much it was hurting. "Here's something that we can use for sacrifice," she told the others. "We can knot it and put it around our waists and offer the pain." Even at night they did not take off those pieces of knotted cord. Our Lady, in the September apparitions, had to tell them not to wear the cord at night.

What a contrast between these emulators of the saints and youth of today, who only seek comfort, pleasure and amusement!

OUR LADY AND THE MISSIONS

Having been called to missionary work and having experienced for many years in Kenya and Ethiopia the life and needs pertaining to missions, I would like to consider the apparitions to Lucia, Jacinta and Francisco in a missionary dimension. The children were invited to look beyond their little world, made of innocence and simplicity, and to see a world with its many problems and difficulties and to redeem it by prayer and sacrifice.

We have heard many times that we belong to a Church that is missionary by its very nature; that the world at large, not only our little personal world, must be our concern and field of action; that all Christians have to be more conscious of themselves as missionaries. The faith we have gratuitously received has to be shared with others in order to remain vibrant and vital. The children of Fatima received that lesson from Our Lady. As a consequence, their personal interests became secondary and their concern went far beyond the world of their playing, their little flock, their parents, their country, to a world always in need of redemption and resurrection.

The message of Fatima and the call of the children have a meaning for all of us. We are reminded by Our Lady of Fatima that all Christians must do the work of Christ in the world—leading all humankind into the Kingdom of God. Fatima reminds us especially of our responsibility to bring Christ to the entire world through prayer, penance and active apostolic work on behalf of the poor and abandoned.

Francisco and Jacinta, declared "venerable" by Pope John Paul II on May 13, 1989, will help us through their example and intercession to become zealous missionaries in our response to the Fatima message. Lucia, hidden in Carmel, will help us through her life of prayer and penance to work strenuously for the conversion of the world to Christ.

Mary: Catechist at Fatima

Rev. Frederick L. Miller

THE MINISTRY OF THE WORD IN OUR TIMES

The last words Jesus spoke to his Apostles before his Ascension into heaven are recorded in the Gospel of St. Matthew: "All authority in heaven and earth has been given to me. Go, therefore, make disciples of all the nations; baptize them in the name of the Father and of the Son and of the Holy Spirit, and teach them to observe all the commands I gave you. And know that I am with you always; yes, to the end of time." (Mt 28: 18–20).

Through these words Christ commissioned the Apostles and their successors to take up as their own his mission of preaching and teaching the Gospel. This task, upon which the very life of the Church depends, has come to be called the ministry of the Word of God.

It is through the instrumentality of the preaching of Chirst's word that people turn from sin to faith in the living God. Through the preaching of the Word, individuals are integrated into the life of the Church and led to the source and summit of her life, the celebration of the Eucharistic Sacrifice. Also, through constant reflection upon the Word of Christ, the faithful glow in conversion to the Lord, and are, thereby, prepared for the vision of God in heaven.

The Church's proclamation of the Word of God is profoundly Trinitarian in essence. The Father wills that his Son be preached and adhered to in faith and charity. Consequently, the Ministry of the Word is one of the most significant manifestations and experiences of the Father's merciful love for his children. When Christ is preached He becomes present through the Word and draws all people through Himself to the Father. The preaching of the Word also "summons" the presence of the Holy Spirit, who, in the words of Vatican II's Constitution on Divine Revelation, *Dei Verbum*, "moves the heart (of the hearer) and converts it to God, opens the eyes of the mind and makes it easy for all to accept and believe the truth. The same Holy Spirit constantly perfects faith by his gifts, so that Divine Revelation may be more and more profoundly understood." (*DV, No. 5*).

The Church delineates four forms of the Ministry of the Word of God. Each form has its own finality and methodology. Each form is distinct yet intimately related to the others:

1. **Evangelization** is the initial proclamation and explanation of Christ, Son of God and Savior. It is the announcement of the saving death and resurrection of the Lord that includes a call to faith, conversion and baptism (cf. Acts 2: 14–41 and Mk 1:15).[1]

2. **Catechesis** is instruction aimed at deepening the life of faith and conversion to Christ. In the words of the *General Catechetical Directory*, catechetics "is intended to make men's faith become living, conscious and active, through the light of instruction" (cf. *GCD*, Nos. 14 and 17).

   Traditionally, catechetics has been understood as the pedagogic explanation of the rudiments or articles of

Catholic Faith and morality under the general headings of the Apostles' Creed, the Ten Commandments, the Sacraments and Sacrifice of the Church and personal prayer.[2] Recent authors have rightly stressed the formational dimensions of catechetics as well as the instructional aspects.

3. **Liturgical Preaching** fosters adherence to Christ, provides ongoing instruction in Christian living and disposes to deeper Eucharistic union with the Lord.

4. **Theology** is the systematic treatment and scientific analysis of the truths of the Faith.

Ideally speaking, in areas where a Christian culture continues to operate, children are evangelized by their parents at home. The parents develop the child's growth in faith through catechesis. This instruction is then supplemented by the Church's catechetical and pre-sacramental programs. Liturgical preaching aims at perfecting Christian life. It is meant to sustain the faith handed on in catechesis throughout a person's lifetime. In the past, at least, few of the faithful have had direct contact with the theological form of the Ministry of the Word. Today there is a felicitous interest among many Catholic people in Sacred Scripture, as well as in dogmatic, moral and spiritual theology.

The point that I want to make and underscore, however, is this: *Cathechesis is the foundational form of the Church's Minstry of the Word.*[3] What comprehending concepts (reading, writing and rudimentary mathematics) is to natural learning, the subject matter of catechesis (the articles of Catholic Faith and morality) is to believing and Christian living.

A person defectively evangelized or not evangelized at all is unprepared for catechetical teaching. The instruction will be senseless. The uncatechized person, in turn, is unprepared to live the Christian life. For him any religious discourse, whether liturgical preaching or theology, will be basically incomprehensible and pointless. We may affirm that the catechetical form of the Ministry of the Word, preceded by careful evangelization and developed by liturgical preaching, insures the health and vigor of the life of the Church and contributes immensely to an individual's salvation.

Of course, the work of evangelization and catechesis is never easy. It was not such for Peter and the Apostles, for Augustine of Canterbury or Patrick of Ireland, for Isaac Jogues, John Neumann or Mother Seton. However, no work is more essential in the life of the Church, as is evidenced in the lives of the saints.

In our time the Church faces many serious difficulties in communicating the Word of God. Some of these difficulties are explained at the very beginning of the *General Catechetical Directory*, issued by the Holy See in 1971: the breakdown of Christian culture and the development of societies based on secular humanism; the ideologies of consumerism and hedonism; religious indifferentism and relativism; widespread religious ignorance; a resurgence of paganism, satanism, militant materialism and dogmatic atheism.

Allow me to present a dramatic historical illustration that synthesizes the various hostile forces we are discussing. It is reported that on May 13, 1917, a sizable group of children and their catechist were brutally slaughtered by the agents of Lenin as a catechetical lesson was in progress in a Catholic church in Moscow.[4] This vicious attack on the Church graphically symbolizes the forces in the modern world that seek to silence the proclamation of the Word of God—especially to the young.

Tertullian in the first Christian centuries stated: "Christians are not born. They are made." The Church has always understood the absolute necessity of evangelizing and catechizing young children. Through this work Christians are formed by the Spirit and the Church. The enemies of Christ's Church understand this point quite well—perhaps better than many of the Church's members. Hence, the first attack of atheistic materialism upon the Church took place in a catechism class. The Word of God was silenced, or so it was thought.

On that very day, perhaps at the very hour of the diabolical slaughter of these innocents, Mary, the Mother of God, came visibly into our world. She came as she had come centuries before to the temple of Jerusalem, heavy-hearted, grieving, in search of her lost child (cf. Lk 2: 42–50). This time she came to three young, illiterate children in Portugal. She came on May 13, 1917, to begin a series of catechetical instructions for the children and, through them, for the entire Church.

In reality, Mary came in search of all her children, redeemed in the precious blood of her only Son, who had already set themselves on the road of rejection of God and rebellion against his Church—on the road that leads to eternal damnation. She came as a Mother to bring the light of Jesus into the darkness of atheism, rebellion and despair which characterizes the so-called modern era of human history.

Who better than Mary is able to lead the people of the twentieth century back to Christ? She was the first person to who the Father revealed the mystery of the Son. She was the first to know, love and serve Him. She was also the first person to be catechized by Christ. Consider this simple fact: The twelve disciples lived with Christ for barely three years. Mary lived with Him ten times longer than they did. She lived under the same roof with the Son of God for thirty years.

In his letter on catechetical instructions entitled *Catechesi Tradendae*, Pope John Paul II extols Mary as the first disciple ("disciple" means student) of Christ and hence the model teacher or catechist of other disciples:

> Mary was the first of Christ's disciples. She was the first in time, because even when she found her adolescent Son in the temple, she received lessons from Him that she kept carefully in her heart (Lk 2:51). She was the first disciple above all else because no one has been "taught by God" (Jn 6:45) to such depth. There are good grounds for the statement made at the synod of bishops on catechetics that Mary is a "living catechism" and the "Mother and model of cathechists."[5]

During her life on earth and even now in heaven, Mary accomplishes through her intercession and interventions what every good catechist seeks to do: Mary leads people to know, love and serve her Divine Son.

It is my task to investigate the catechetical content of the message of Fatima. I shall begin by examining the message itself as it is related to the memoirs of Sister Lucia, the surviving seer of Fatima. In this context, I shall single out a few of the spiritual fruits of the message in the lives of the children who first put it into practice. In particular, I shall look at Jacinta and Francisco, who were declared "venerable" by Pope John Paul II on May 13, 1989. I shall use as my major resource the perceptive journal of Sister Lucia that is published in English under the title *Fatima in Lucia's Own Words*.[6] Finally, I shall draw some practical conclusions from the catechetical content of the message of Fatima for our contemporary ecclesial situation.

THE CATECHETICAL APPROACH OF OUR LADY AT FATIMA

Jacinta, Francisco and Lucia were prepared catechetically for the apparitions of Our Blessed Mother by frequent communication with the angels. On each occasion the angel, in Lucia's words, "appeared in the form of a young man, transparent and much brighter than crystal pierced by the rays of the sun." During the first visitation the angel told the children: "Fear not. I am the Angel of Peace. Pray with me." Kneeling and then bowing his head to the ground, the angel taught the children a prayer of adoration and supplication: "My God, I believe, I adore, I trust and I love Thee. I ask pardon for those who do not believe, do not adore, do not trust and do not love Thee."

During the second visit, the angel again directed the children to adore God and to love their neighbor. "Pray a great deal.

The Hearts of Jesus and Mary have designs of mercy on you. Offer up prayers and sacrifices to the Most High." Lucia asked: "How are we to make sacrifices?" The angel answered: "Make everything you do a sacrifice and offer it as an act of reparation for the sins by which God is offended, and in supplication for the conversion of sinners. Bring peace to your country in this way. Above all, accept and bear with submission the sufferings sent you by Our Lord."

In the final apparition, some six months before Our Lady's appearance, the Angel of Peace taught the children to offer themselves with Jesus to the Father in the Mass and to adore the Blessed Sacrament. The angel, bearing the Eucharistic Species, adored Christ with the children and gave them Holy Communion. Again, the angel taught them a prayer that became part of their daily relationship with God:

> Most Holy Trinity, Father, Son and Holy Spirit, I adore Thee profoundly. I offer Thee the most precious Body, Blood, Soul and Divinity of Jesus Christ present in all the tabernacles of the world, in reparation for the outrages, sacrileges and indifference by which He is offended. And through the infinite merits of his most Sacred Heart, and of the Immaculate Heart of Mary, I beg the conversion of poor sinners.

Then the angel gave the Host to Lucia, and the Contents of the chalice to Jacinta and Francisco. For Jacinta and Francisco, seven and nine years old, this was their first Holy Communion. As he gave them Communion, he said: "Take and drink the Body and Blood of Jesus Christ horribly outraged by ungrateful men. Repair their crime and console your God."

It is interesting to note that Francisco was not aware that he had received Holy Communion from the hands of the angel. However, by the work of the Holy Spirit, he recognized and adored the Real Presence in his soul. A few days after the event he asked: "The angel gave you Holy Communion, Lucia, but what was it he gave Jacinta and me?" She replied, "It was Holy Communion too. Didn't you see that it was the Blood that fell from the Host?" Francisco answered: "I felt that God was within me, but I did not know how."

Lucia relates the impact the apparitions of the angel and his "catechesis" had on her and on her younger cousins: "The angel's words made a deep impression on our minds, like a light making us understand who God is, how He loves us and desires to be loved, as well as the value of sacrifice; how pleasing it is to Him and how, on account of it, He grants the grace of conversion to sinners."

Already the children had been well instructed by heaven. The work of the angel was to prepare the children for the great catechetical lessons of the Mother of God.

On May 13, 1917, the children saw the Blessed Mother for the first time. Lucia relates her first impression of the Mother of God: "We beheld a lady all dressed in white. She was more brilliant than the sun, and radiated a light more clear and intense than a crystal glass filled with sparkling water when the rays of the burning sun shine through it."

The vision of the Blessed Mother was the first and, in a sense, the most important of all the catechetical lessons. The children spoke frequently of her beauty, her kindness and especially of the wonderful light that shone all about her. They knew immediately that she was from heaven and that she radiated the light of God Himself. They knew, without being able to articulate it, that Mary existed in a glorified body and she shared physically in Christ's triumph over sin and death. Her beauty, in fact, was his work within her—the mystery of the Immaculate Conception. The children were not "annihilated" by her presence as they had been by the Angel of Peace. Rather, they felt the joy and security of the presence of a Mother. They experienced her "fullness of grace" in a maternal way. She brought with her a profound experience of God's presence and love. Her spiritual motherhood was immediately evident to the children.

The first thing Mary did for the children was to steal from

them their natural fear of death. They discovered in her that life exists beyond the confines of this world, beyond the barrier of the grave. Mary told them: "I am from heaven." Lucia, speaking for the three, said: "Will I go to heaven too? And Jacinta and Francisco?" Mary told them that they would. From that moment, the children no longer feared death and, in fact, began to long to be with God and Our Lady in heaven.

In the apparitions the children experienced the Holy Trinity in Mary, or, to be exact, in the light that emanated from Mary's heart. In reference to the May apparition, Lucia states: "Our Lady opened her hands for the first time, communicating to us a light so intense that, as it streamed from her hands, its rays penetrated our hearts and the innermost depths of our souls, making us see oursleves in God, *Who is that light,* more clearly than we see ourselves in the best of mirrors. Then, moved by an interior impulse that was also communicated to us, we fell to our knees repeating in our hearts: 'O Most Blessed Trinity, I adore you. My God, my God, I love you in the Most Blessed Sacrament.' "

This phenomenon of experiencing God in the light of Mary was repeated more strongly in the June apparition. Lucia notes: "As Our Lady spoke the words 'I will be your refuge and the way that will lead you to God,' she opened her hands and for the second time she communicated to us the rays of that same intense light. We saw oursleves in this light, as it were, immersed in God. In the front of the palm of Our Lady's right hand was a heart encircled by thorns which pierced it. We understood that this was the Immaculate Heart of Mary, outraged by the sins of humanity, and seeking reparation."

Francisco recognized and sought to articulate the phenomenon of God manifested through Mary's Immaculate Heart: "These people are so happy just because you [Lucia] told them that Our Lady wants the Rosary said, and that you are to learn to read. How would they feel if they only knew what she showed to us in God, in her Immaculate Heart, in that great light?" On another occasion, Francisco said to Lucia: "I loved seeing the angel, but I loved still more seeing Our Lady. What I loved most of all was to see Our Lord in that light from Our Lady which penetrated our hearts."

We may affirm that God, in permitting the children to experience directly the mysteries of Mary's Immaculate Conception, her spiritual maternity and Assumption into heaven, communicated to them a deep knowledge of themselves. They described the "light" as penetrating their hearts. It caused them to know themselves in God. From this developed their great hatred of sin and their desire to live in such a way as to always be pleasing to God. The Lord also communicated to the children a "connatural" knowledge of Himself and eternal life. They not only knew about God, they knew God in a deeply interior and personal way. Through this knowledge they came to love Him directly and in others. The Immaculate Heart of Mary instantaneously weaned them from any fear of God, death or spiritual reality.

In the July apparition, Our Lady gave the children a momentary vision of hell. Lucia's description is well worth our careful consideration:

> Our Lady opened her hands once more, as she had done during the two previous months. The rays of light seemed to penetrate the earth and we saw, as it were, a sea of fire. Plunged in this fire were demons and souls in human form, like transparent burning embers, all blackened or burnished like bronze, floating about in the conflagration, now raised into the air by the flames that issued from within themselves together with great clouds of smoke, now falling back on every side like sparks and in huge fires, without weight or equilibrium amid shrieks and groans of pain and despair which horrified us and made us tremble with fear. The demons could be distinguished by their terrifying and repellent likeness to frightful and unknown animals, black and transparent like burning coals. Terrified and as if to plead for succor, we looked at Our Lady,

who said so kindly and so sadly: "You have seen hell where poor sinners go. To save them, God wishes to establish in the world devotion to my Immaculate Heart."

Lucia admitted that she and her cousins would have died of fright had not Our Lady promised them heaven in the previous apparitions.

In the subsequent three visions, Mary as a master teacher, repeats and reviews her simple instruction. She reinforces the love of God and neighbor in the children. She communicates a knowledge of self, of God, of the iniquity of sin. She calls for faith, conversion, prayer, and vicarious penance.

In response to Mary's assurance that they would be able to help save souls from hell through prayer and penance, the three children placed themselves wholeheartedly at the service of Christ and his redemptive work. With driving force and heroic effort they set as their goals consoling God and saving sinners. Numerous instances of their response to Our Lady's catechesis are recorded by Lucia.

Jacinta's main concern was to perform acts of love and voluntary penance to save sinners from the fires of hell. Jacinta also developed a very special love and concern for the Holy Father. She always included him and his intentions in her prayers and sacrifices. In the July apparition the Blessed Virgin had told the children that "the Holy Father will have much to suffer."

When Jacinta was in the prison cell of Ourem, surrounded by hardened criminals and threatened with torture and death, she prayed: "O my Jesus! This is for love of you, for the conversion of sinners, *for the Holy Father* and in reparation for the sins committed against the Immaculate Heart of Mary." Jacinta grew to love the Holy Father and to sense his spiritual identification with Christ as Head of the Church. She intuited that the pope shares Jesus' agony over sin and therefore gave herself to heroic acts of penance to save sinners from hell and thereby to console the pope.

Through the sorrow on the face of Our Lady, Francisco

intuited the agony in the heart of Christ, caused by the eternal loss of even one soul in the fires of hell. The boy's main concern was to console Jesus in the Blessed Sacrament.

Lucia states: "Francisco was a boy of few words. Whenever we prayed or offered sacrifices, he preferred to go apart and hide, even from Jacinta and myself. If I asked him: 'Francisco, which do you like better—to console Our Lord or to convert sinners, so that no more souls will go to hell?' 'I would rather console Our Lord,' he responded. 'Didn't you notice how sad Our Lady was that last month when she said that people must not offend Our Lord any more for He is already much offended? I would like to console Our Lord and after that to convert sinners.' "

Francisco's great love for the Blessed Sacrament motivated him to spend large segments of his day in front of the tabernacle. Obviously, this love for the Eucharistic Christ, whom Francisco called "Hidden Jesus," is another component of the Fatima catechesis and an important lesson for our time.

In her journal Lucia writes: "Sometimes on our way to school, as soon as we reached Fatima, Francisco would say to me: 'Listen! You go to school and I'll stay here in the church close to the hidden Jesus. It's not worth my while learning to read, as I'll be going to heaven very soon. On your way home come here and call me.' "

Elsewhere Lucia states: "Later when Francisco fell ill, he often told me, when I called in to see him on my way to school, 'Look, go to the church and give my love to the hidden Jesus. What hurts me most is that I cannot go there myself and stay awhile with the hidden Jesus.' "

In a homily preached at the Shrine of the Immaculate Heart of Mary in Washington, New Jersey on May 13, 1989, Cardinal Edouard Gagnon, President of the Pontifical Council for the Family, announced that Pope John Paul II had declared Jacinta and Francisco "venerable" that very day. The cardinal noted that the Church has proclaimed the children's virtue heroic not because they had seen the Blessed Virgin nor the angel nor the

Miracle of the Sun. "No, Jacinta and Francisco are venerable," the Cardinal said, "because they responded heroically to Our Lady's pleas for personal conversion, prayer and reparation at the price of great personal sacrifices."[7]

This response, of course, bears testimony to the work of the sanctifying spirit of God in their young souls. Our Lady, with all of the gentle care of a mother, presented the rudimentary articles of the faith to the children. As a master catechist, she appealed to their senses and deepest human emotions. In this way the truth of the Gospel entered their minds and hearts and elicited a response of charity.

From the moment of the first apparition, the children experienced Mary's tender love for them. Hence, the vision of the Immaculate Heart! In the light emanating from her heart, the children experienced God whose true name is LOVE. Mary led them to a deep love for the Holy Trinity. Furthermore, the sadness of Jesus and Mary moved the children to want to do something restoral to console the good God.

In the vision of hell, Mary again appealed to the children's senses and deepest sympathies. Besides engendering in them a horror of sin and a desire to preserve their baptismal innocence the Virgin inspired the children to assist "poor sinners" by prayer and voluntary sacrifices. Obviously the children had no understanding whatsoever of Mary's words about communism. They did understand, however, that people would spend eternity in hellfire because of their willful revolt against Almighty God and his commandments. After all, they had seen people in hell! They knew that they must help.

Their desire to spend their lives saving sinners had two essentially related motives: Jesus, they knew, suffered for all and desired salvation for everyone. His deepest and most bitter agony on the cross was caused by the prospect of the loss of even one soul redeemed in his precious blood. After the apparitions the only motive that directed the lives of the children was the desire to console Jesus who was so wounded by sin and human indifference. Directly related to this sensitivity to the

Heart of Christ was their simple wish to help people who were in dire trouble as a result of their sins.

It is quite clear that Mary, in the course of her Fatima apparitions, simply taught the children how to practice Christ's "Law of Love": "You must love the Lord your God with all your heart, with all your soul, and with all your mind. This is the greatest and the first commandment. The second resembles it: 'You must love your neighbor as yourself' " (Mt 22: 37–38).

THE CATECHETICAL CONTENT OF THE FATIMA MESSAGE

For the sake of clarity allow me to list the major catechetical truths communicated to the children by Our Lady in the six apparitions that took place between May 13 and October 13, 1917. I shall omit here the points of "prophecy" made by the Blessed Mother. Although prophesies are important in themselves and are an integral part of the message of Fatima, we must neither forget nor obscure the essential components of the message: faith, conversion to Christ and reparation.

1. God the Father's merciful love for every human person is definitively revealed in the gift of his Son. Many people in the twentieth century are indifferent to and even antagonistic toward Christ.

2. The mission of Christ is essentially redemptive. Christ came into the world to offer his life in sacrifice for the salvation of all people.

3. In Christ, God suffers as a result of sin. In Christ also, God loves mankind with a human heart and yearns for human love in return.

4. In his conversion from mortal sin, man begins to love the good God. This love continues and grows to perfection as he desires to make reparation for his own sins and the sins of others through acts of charity.

5. When a Christian surrenders himself unreservedly to the Lord, he consoles Jesus and satiates his thirst for souls.

6. Through the sanctifying power of the Holy Spirit working in the Church and in intimate communion with Christ, the Christian becomes "perfectly willing to spend all and to be expended in the interest of souls" (2 Cor 12:15) and "makes up in his own body what has still to be undergone by Christ for the sake of his body the Church" (Col 1:24). In other words, every Christian is called to give himself unreservedly to Christ's redeeming work. He does this by conversion, fidelity to daily duty, prayer (especially the Rosary), acts of charity, acceptance of sufferings permitted by God and voluntary penances.

7. The Church, the Mystical Body of Christ, following Mary as model and guide, unites her self-sacrifice to Christ's and becomes his co-worker in the world. The collective suffering of the Church as a whole, and of each Christian, joined to Christ's suffering, brings the saving grace of the Lord to souls. The Church's active role in the application of the grace of Redemption is perhaps the major emphasis of the Fatima message. (Please note that this theme is conspicuously absent from many expressions of contemporary ecclesiology and is all but forgotten in many quarters as an essential component of the Church's ascetical-mystical doctrine. This fatal deficiency leads either to the denial or the devaluation of the Eucharist as the redemptive sacrifice of Christ and his Church. Hence, the need for Eucharistic reparation is at the heart of the Fatima catechesis.)

8. Every aspect of spirit and the spiritual world is underscored in the Fatima message: the Trinity, angels, demons, the existence of the immortal human soul; heaven, hell and purgatory.

9. Fatima affirms the essential importance of the Vicar of Christ in the daily life of the Church as well as the pope's mystic identification with Christ, the crucified bridegroom of the Church.

10. Fatima unambiguously reaffirms the doctrine of hellfire (the pain of sense) and the real possibility of eternal damnation.

11. The Christian's union with Christ in his suffering, death and resurrection leads to perfect union with Him in heaven; to the resurrection of the flesh on the last day and to the life of the world to come.

12. Mary reveals that her spiritual Motherhood is the way to fidelity to Christ and eternal life. Through total consecration to Mary, the Christian accepts and benefits from her Motherhood in the spirit.

A cursory analysis of the these fundamental catechetical truths leads one to see that Our Lady presented the children with the truth about God (the Creed), the way to respond to God in love (the Commandments), as well as the means to conversion and growth in sanctity (the Mass, the Sacraments and personal prayer). The message of Fatima is unmistakably Theocentric and Christocentric.

The catechetical teaching of Mary at Fatima was perfectly adapted to the capacity of the children, yet able to benefit every member of the Church, including the most intellectual and sophisticated.

The scriptural doctrine of the "two ways" is at the heart of the Fatima message. Each person must make a choice: the way to death or the way to life; unbelief and rebellion or faith and conversion; self or Christ; hell or heaven. Through the innocent children of Fatima, Mary has asked the Church in the twentieth century to be very conscious of the choice, which by necessity, confronts every person, even the very young: the choice of eternal life or eternal death.

CONCLUSIONS

As I attempted to unravel the catechetical content of the message of Fatima in the preparation of this article, I realized that Our Lady's message is profound and comprehensive. I began to suspect that very few have even begun to plummet the depths of this heavenly communication. The Fatima event, I am sure, will remain wrapped in holy mystery, enfolded as it is in the inscrutability of God, prophecy and Providence.

We must be very careful not to take one part of the message and allow it to overshadow and obscure the full truth of Fatima. I fear that some have concentrated only on the secret, the collegial consecration, the practical details of the conversion of Russia or the various phenomena such as the solar miracle or the vision of hell and by so doing miss or render myopic the Blessed Virgin's central teaching: **The application of the grace of the Redemption is accomplished through the Church— the Mystical Body of Christ. By giving himself or herself unreservedly to God through conversion, prayer, sacrifice and other acts of charity, each member of the Church is called to be an instrument of Christ in the work of saving souls.**

When our Holy Father journeyed to Fatima in May 1982, one year to the day after the attack on his life, he preached a magnificent homily. Situating the message of Fatima in the context of God's public revelation, the Holy Father said: "If the

Church has accepted the message of Fatima, it is above all because the message contains a truth and a call whose basic content is the truth and the call of the Gospel itself."[8]

Obviously, Our Lady came to Fatima to combat the atheism, rebellion and materialism of the modern world. She came from God to save souls from unbelief, sin, and ultimately from hellfire. She came, begging all believers to join Christ in his work of redemption by living faith-filled and holy lives.

The conclusion that I draw from our brief excursion into the catechetical content of Fatima is this: **Fatima calls all Catholics to be deeply renewed in faith, conversion and spiritual life.**

Our Lady's message should inspire all to know the faith in a more mature and comprehensive way; to study the content of the Creed, the moral law, the social teachings of the Church; to come to a better understanding of the Holy Eucharist and the other sacraments as well as of Christian prayer, liturgical and devotional. Through this study of the content of the Sacred Deposit of the Faith carried out in communion of mind and heart with the Vicar of Christ, each Catholic will become equipped to be an effective evangelist and catechist, each in his or her own sphere of influence.

In a yet unpublished paper, Father René Laurentin notes that private revelation usually highlights an aspect or several aspects of the original and normative Deposit of Faith and Morality. He observes that the elements of faith stressed in private revelations are often those eclipsed and very much needed at a particular juncture of history.

It is interesting and beneficial, I believe, to consider the twelve catechetical points listed above in light of the Ministry of the Word, especially the catechetical form of that ministry in its contemporary format. This exercise will lead you to realize how desperately we and especially the young need the message of Fatima today.

Furthermore, Fatima challenges Catholics to seek the perfection of Christian Charity. In Chapter V of *Lumen Gentium,* the Dogmatic Constitution on the Church of the Second Vatican

Council, the Fathers of the Council taught that each of the baptized is called by God to seek Christian perfection through the careful observance of God's law of love and the practice of the evangelical counsels of poverty, chastity and obedience according to his state of life.

I believe that it may rightly be said that the "Universal Call to Holiness" is the core of the doctrine of the Second Vatican Council. It is the special work of the Holy Spirit today. The evil spirit's particular work in our day seems to keep Catholics distracted with superficial issues so they never realize or implement this teaching.

Through Jacinta, Franciscso and Lucia, many others heard and responded to the "Universal Call to Holiness" over seventy years ago, fifty-five years prior to the Second Vatican Council.

In his 1984 consecration of the world to the Immaculate Heart of Mary, the Holy Father thanked all those in our times who actively seek Christian perfection:

> Blessed are all those souls who obey the call of eternal love. Blessed are all those who, day after day, with undiminished generosity, accept your invitation, O Mother, to do what your Jesus tells them (cf. Jn 2:5) and give to the Church and the world a serene testimony of lives inspired by the Gospel.[9]

In this same consecration the Holy Father challenged all Catholics to heed Our Lady's call—Vatican II's call to Gospel holiness:

> How pained we are by all the things in the Church and in each one of us that are opposed to holiness and consecration. How pained we are that the invitation to repentance, conversion, and prayer has not met with the acceptance that it should have received. How pained we are that many share so coldly in Christ's work of redemption. That 'what is lacking in Christ's affliction' (Col 1:24) is so insufficiently completed in our flesh.[10]

The unambiguous doctrinal and moral teaching of the Church is the only path to authentic holiness. Unfortunately, many today are being denied this undiluted Catholic doctrine and morality especially in its catechetical form. It becomes inceasingly evident that this sound teaching is often not part of the formation of future priests. Until the faith, in its integrity, and especially those elements of the faith stressed by Our Lady of Fatima are properly reintegrated into the content and praxis of the Ministry of the Word at the parish level, people will continue to fall away from the Church and view Christianity as a banal philosophical abstraction. They will neither know God in a personal way nor understand how to please Him. They will be spiritually paralyzed and unable to take even the first step on the road to Christian perfection. Mary's catechesis at Fatima includes the elements of authentic Christian spiritual formation so vitally needed today.

In the June apparition, Our Lady said to Lucia, "I will be your refuge and the way that leads you to God." Might these words be meant not only for Lucia but for the Church in the twentieth century? Perseverance in the Catholic Faith, the spread of the faith through the Ministry of the Word, and personal growth in holiness must proceed today under the motherly guidance of Mary. Consecration to her Immaculate Heart is the way to fidelity to Christ in our times. For Christ to be known, loved and served in the world today—for Christ to reign—the work of the Church must proceed under the guidance of Our Lady. At Fatima she is revealed as the model of the Church's catechetical ministry for all times but in particular for our times.

Pope John Paul II, in his encyclical letter *Redemptoris Mater*, notes that Mary is the way to Christ and Mother of our life of faith. The Holy Father's words, describe in capsule form Mary's catechetical "course" given to the Christian world at Fatima:

> For every Christian, for every human being, Mary is the one who first "believed" and precisely with her faith as Spouse and Mother she wishes to act upon all those who entrust themselves to her as her children. And it is

well known that the more her children persevere and progress in this attitude, the nearer Mary leads them to the unsearchable riches of Christ (Eph 3:8).

Many have returned to the faith and the sacraments in our times through contact with the Fatima story. For them and for many others, who have never abandoned the life of grace, the Fatima message remains a powerful means of growth in the spiritual life. Might we not hope that the Holy Spirit through the message of Fatima will now raise up an army of zealous evangelists and catechists of the Catholic Faith? Nothing would seem more consistent with the message than this. So, let us pray and begin to work.

Footnotes

1. Pope Paul VI, "Evangelization in the Modern World" (*Evangelii Nuntiandi*), 1975.
2. *See,* The Sacred Congregation of the Clergy, *The General Catechetical Directory (Directorium Catechisticum Generale)*, 1971 and Pope John Paul II on *Catechesis in Our Time* (Catechesi Tradendae), 1979 for two recent magisterial statements on authentic catechetical teaching. These and other catechetical documents of the twentieth century are published in *Teaching the Catholic Faith Today; Twentieth Century Catechetical Documents of the Holy See* (Boston: Daughters of St. Paul, 1982). Note the lucid introduction to this compendium by the Rev. Msgr. Eugene Kevane.
3. *See,* Ratzinger, Joseph Cardinal, "Sources and Transmissions of the Faith," *Communio* (Spring 1983) pp. 17-35, for an excellent and contemporary survey of the Church's "method" of transmitting the content of Sacred Scripture and the importance of the format of The Roman Catechism.
4. Pelletier, A.A., Rev. Joseph, *The Sun Danced At Fatima* (New York: Doubleday Image Books, 1983), p. 30.
5. *Catechesi Tradendi,* No. 73.
6. Sister Mary Lucia of the Immaculate Heart, *Fatima in Lucia's Own Words,* (Fatima, Portugal: Postulation Center, 1983).
7. Gagnon, Edouard Cardinal, "The Triumph of Mary in Jacinta and Francisco Marto, *SOUL* Magazine, (Vol. XL, September-October 1989), pp. 6–7.
8. Pope John Paul II, "And From That Hour . . . " (Washington, N.J.: AMI Press, 1989), p. 7.
9. *Ibid.,* p. 20.
10. *Ibid.,* p. 19.

Sacred Scripture and the Message of Fatima

Rev. René Laurentin

METHODOLOGY

The study of apparitions proceeds from broad methodological principles that are essentially biblical. They consist of the following:

Revelation and Specific Revelations

Revelation ended with the death of the last Apostle. The Apostles were competent to transmit Christ's Revelation: a Revelation that was complete and sufficient for the salvation of humanity. This Revelation can be articulated more clearly in a more orderly and explicit manner by church tradition, but nothing can be added to the Sacred Deposit of Faith as revealed by Christ and transmitted through Apostolic tradition.

Consequently, "private revelations," the term used to characterize heavenly communications after the period of Normative Revelation cannot add anything to Divine Revelation (properly so-called). If a particular apparition claimed to introduce a new doctrine, we would have to say of it what Paul said to the Galatians: "Even if an angel from heaven were to bring you a gospel other than the one I preached to you, let him be anathema" (Gal 1:8).

Problems and Difficulties

The methodology used here will therefore be the one I developed in The Meaning of Lourdes (Paris 1955)—a methodology that was accepted by the Holy See and to some extent appropriated by Pius XII on the occasion of the centenary of Lourdes in 1958: "An apparition is nothing but a reminder of revelation, for the purpose of opening our deaf ears to hear and helping our blind eyes to see the things we have forgotten; to reawaken our sleepy memories." An authentic private revelation is therefore always a fragmentary message. Its function is to arouse an *anamnesis* (memory) of the misunderstood revelation. It enlightens the revelation, gives it life, renders it explicit and current, always in relation to a particular time and place. It is a timely reminder of what we know, or at least should know, about the revelation of Christ transmitted by the tradition of the Church.

Private revelations, the type received in apparitions, are accordingly like a dot matrix of the full, constitutive Divine Revelation. To understand these generally laconic and limited private messages, they must be applied over the original and normative revelation like a transparent overlay that highlights or clarifies the image. This can be accomplished by following the two channels of the unique revelation:

Scripture (in written form, fixed during the apostolic generation);

Tradition (oral transmission of Revelation, including Scripture, by the channel of the Church).

We will therefore seek to identify which elements of Divine Revelation are chosen and highlighted by the message of Fatima; where they are located in the body of revelation; how they help us better to understand, to deepen our knowledge of, to authenticate, to complete and even to rectify the private revelation.

One might hesitate to use this last term. If it is the Virgin who is speaking, there can hardly be any question of "rectifying." But the message of Fatima, like any message, is transmitted by men who are not infallible, who have their limits. In view of this, it calls for what we refer to as "hermeneutics," or an interpretation; for the charism of the visionary sets in motion his personal activity and creativity. The exercise of this prophetic function is therefore limited and may be subject to errors of interpretation or explanation.

It is therefore not a question of setting up an external and negative critique, such as that of Father Dhanis (a Dutch theologian of some repute, since he was once rector of the Gregorianum and one of the foremost authorities of the *Holy Office*). It is merely a question of defining what is truly essential in the message of Fatima, of placing in context its particular or even particularist elements, such as the time, the place, the culture and the youthfulness of the visionaries: these children may have placed their own imprint on the transmission of the message.

Referring the revelations to Revelation consequently underscores the limits of private revelations and may seem to deny them any intrinsic value. Yet these messages are not merely repetitive recordings. They make the Normative Revelation real or actual in terms of the needs of a particular time and place. Revelation finds therein a renewed meaning and value, with distinctive, particular applications.

This methodological rule is all the more essential since the message of Fatima is not free of problems, theologians have already discussed. The more significant problems with the message are several. First, the pain of God, of Christ, and of the Virgin in heaven (which the visionaries talk about) has puzzled some. It is to be explained by the synchronism of eternity with every moment in time, for Christ's cross and Mary's compassion are synchronized with the eternal *I* of the Son of God, and the integrity of time appropriated into eternity; but also by the fact that God is not apathetic or indifferent, even though He is above any corruptibility.

Second, the consecration to the Immaculate Heart poses a problem. Strictly speaking, there can be consecration only to God and by God, as consecration is our divinization. Christian consecration, which is essentially the baptismal grace, flows from a divine election and anointing of the Holy Spirit. It is God alone who consecrates. This is very well expressed in Jn 17: 17–19 (cf. 10:36), "Consecrate them [the verb is *hagiazein*] in the truth, as I consecrate myself."

It is clearly God who consecrates us. If Christ says that He consecrates *Himself*, it is because He is God. All these facts are based on the Bible. There is an even greater basis to explain this: God is all, man is nothing by himself. Since consecration is divinization, it can come only from God Himself. Similarly, one can adore only God, as the Council specifically stated, and sacrifice can be offered only to Him, for everything belongs to Him. One can never agree to be the absolute property of any creature.

The consecration to the Immcaulate Heart is, therefore, to be understood as an improper use of the word (just as we say that we are consecrating ourselves to business or pleasure). This is true for various reasons. Only Christ, being God, can consecrate Himself. We can only *dispose* ourselves, or offer ourselves to this divinization and consecration, which is definitely God's work. Mary is not the final goal of our consecration. To be more exact, we place ourselves in the hands of Mary, our Mother, by giving ourselves and abandoning ourselves, so that she can dispose us to consecration and turn us over to God, who alone can achieve for us the final goal of divinization.

Other problems with the message of Fatima involve the limitations of the visionaries—their commonplace and peasant culture, their condition as children. Let us not say their lack of culture. They did not have the culture of intellectuals, but they had their own culture—that of a people of faith, rooted in an ancient civilization whose values should not be trivialized. The norms of our culture, even at its theological level, are not the measure of all things. The mark of an evolved culture is not to judge, criticize or despise other cultures, but to respect, understand, and learn from them.

The children of Fatima spoke the language of a popular culture, intellectually underdeveloped, or rather, in the process of development. The methods of presentation are naive and symbolic. They can include theological approximations. They call for a hermeneutic interpretation. This is not an invitation to minimize the importance of Fatima, but rather to enrich or fill out this special message within the very fullness of Divine Revelation. Intercultural and transcultural, but not reductionist, consideration will enable us to appreciate the special meaning of the message.

The keys to such hermeneutical consideration seem to me to involve the following matters. The visionaries were living in a solid and symbolic culture, related to that of the Bible. It is not so much a question of demythologizing biblical teaching or the teaching of Fatima, to reduce it to the abstractions of scholastic thought, but rather to evaluate it in the light of Divine Revelation itself.

The Virgin's discourse with the visionaries must be understood within the religious tradition of the people in those days, formed by the teaching of the catechism. (Of course this teaching was rooted in the scriptural revelation and faithful to it.) She remained very faithful to the catechism and illustrated it in vivid colors, which we would do well to understand in terms of its proper values as well as its limitations.

The peculiarities of the message can be traced to two causes. First, there is the adage of Aristotelian philosophy popularized by Thomas Aquinas: *"Quidquid recipitur ad modum recipientis recipitur.*—Whatever is received is received according to the mode of the receiver" (according to its form, its limits, its capacity).

Second, Fatima involves the adaptation of heaven to the Portuguese language and culture. Anyone who speaks a foreign language knows the difficulty of trying to translate one's speech into another language and another culture. The main attribute of a translator is his ability to grasp the peculiar spirit of the language he is interpreting and to permit the maximum passage of the message from one language into another, one culture into another. That requires interpretations and transpositions where there is no strict equivalence in words, concepts, or turns of phrases between the languages. When God and God's servants, living in the beatific vision, speak at a given time and place, they know how to adapt to that language and culture. They take into account the capacities of the listener.

One must discern in each case what part of the teaching comes from heaven, and what part from the visionary, who received it according to his capacity and interpreted it.

In Fatima, the Virgin spoke Portuguese, just as she spoke the local dialect in Lourdes; she addressed herself to the visionaries according to their language and mental capacities. The visionaries were, in a sense, overwhelmed by this message, which is larger than themselves. Sometimes they hesitated. "It seems to me, if I understood correctly," Lucia would sometimes say. The seers bring into play their own degree of interiorization, of maturity, of interpretation and even of explanation. Questions from inquirers are a source of embarrassment whenever they seek to elicit greater details about the message than what had been received. They often resist such efforts, but always within certain limits, for requests for greater detail have their own degree of legitimacy.

Language and Praxis of the Message

A final difficulty preoccupies or disheartens the theologians who take issue with this particular message of Fatima. This message, whose function is to recall or reactualize the Gospel or a certain component of it, seems at first glance rather superficial and repetitive, which disappoints the professional intellectual.

But the purpose of such messages is not to instruct, much less to impart new, original truths. Their ultimate function is to elicit an understanding that is lived, a *praxis*, in those who receive it. It is important not to get bogged down in the *words* of the message but to grasp the *experience* that this message has elicited—in the visionaries and in God's people. Only on this plane can the message be read and understood, can it manifest its true value, which is a vital value: the value of the love that this message elicits and gives life to. That is what counts, and what will last, the end beyond the means.

It is love that gives value to life. That is true for any married couple living a true and profound love. Every morning is new and filled with the happines of living with the other, of seeing the other again, so that the death of one is for the other the greatest of sufferings. Love determines the cost of life, its very value. And that is even more profoundly true since our life here below is given to learn not only about human love but about divine love which will be perfection revealed at the end of our earthly destiny, in eternal life. The *value* of this experience is that of a *praxis* which enables us to share the very nature of God, that is, the nature of love.

Let us not forget the following principle that appears in the Prologue to the *Summa Theologiae:* "Theology is a science that is not merely speculative, but practical as well." To put it another way, it is a *praxis*, that is, *a body of knowledge meant to build people as individuals and as a community.* Essentially, people can only understand themselves by doing, interacting with others and reflecting. That is a truth of nature, inscribed by the Creator in the very nature of the rational animal who can fulfill his nature only by activity in communion with others.

On a higher plane, it is a principle of Christ's revelation:

> Whoever neglects the least of (my) commandments... will be called the least in the kingdom of heaven.
> And whoever DOES and teaches, he will be great in the kingdom of heaven (Mt 5:19).
> He who hears my words and DOES them will be like a wise man who BUILT his house on rock. Let rain come and wind blow it will not fall, for it is set on rock (Mt 7:24–25).

The first text speaks of "doing" the commandments (and unfortunately it is weakly translated as "putting into practice." both here and in the other texts). The second text speaks of "doing" the words of Christ. A third text, from Jn 3:20, declares: "He who DOES the truth comes into the light."

To "do" the commandments, to "do" the words is in the end "to do" the love of God and of men, for all of the law is summed up in love.

"To do the truth." That is first of all the gift of oneself according to the paradox of the Gospel: "He who would save his life will lose it and he who loses it will save it." That is what Christ did. Here we have both Supper and sacrifice, for love does not seek itself, it loses itself and finds itself again in that very same love within the other, for whom it has agreed to become lost. It finds itself in the reciprocity of the gift.

"To do the truth," to do the love of God and of mankind (as Mother Teresa is doing, for example), is also to build up man according to the law of God.

In the text quoted from St. John (so poorly translated) note well that the Gospel does not use the word "do" (*poieien*, from which comes poetic), but *brassein*: to practice, to exercise evil. One does not *do* that, for evil is nothingness. It is the formula of the gospel praxis that was attained by the visionaries of Fatima and those who are living out its consecration.

It is certainly not a Marxist praxis (although Marx did invent and launch the word itself), but a Christian praxis that is totally different. For the praxis of Marx is a vengeful combat that begins by destroying in order to build up: it manages to destroy but does not succeed in building up, as has been proven in Marxist countries. The gospel praxis builds up love, reconciliation, communion. It builds, not the tower of Babel, but a profound and indestructible work that is completed in heaven. This building is earthly, despite the risks of the cross, but it is also, and even more so, heavenly. It is the *integral building* of the eternal kingdom of God.

Thus were the lives of Francisco and Jacinta built, as an expressway to heaven. Thus is being built, with long-term construction, the life of Lucia. Thus were built around them the lives of those who seek to live the message of Fatima as prayer, as consecration, as sacrifice. That, in the final analysis, is what needs to be deepened.

We have now come full circle to what we said about the prophetic nature of the message. "Prophetic" refers to a word announced to man in the name of God at a moment of time in history, in order to actualize the gift and building of God. For the ultimate aim of apparitions is not to complete the faith by objective information, but to renovate and stimulate it. In that sense it pertains more to hope than to faith. Apparitions and private revelations have more of a practical than speculative nature, as Thomas Aquinas and Cajetan stated. Their function is to regulate conduct and plan the future rather than to unveil truths, as John XXIII recalled in 1959:

> We urge you to listen with simplicity of heart and rightness of spirit to the salutary and always pertinent warnings of the Mother of God. . . . The Roman Pontiffs recommend to the attention of the faithful . . . *the supernatural enlightenments which God vouchsafes to freely pour out on certain privileged souls, not to propose new doctrines but to guide our conduct* [(*non ad novam doctrinam fidei depromedam, sed ad humanorum actuum directiones*) Thomas Aquinas 2, 11 q 174 a 6, ad 3]. Such is certainly the case with apparitions . . . (D. Bertetto, *Acta Mariana*

Johannis PP XXIII, Pas Verlag, 1964, cf. *Documentation catholique* 56, 1959, col. 274–275).

The message of prayer and conversion is a common denominator in all apparitions. Fatima adds to it a message for a world at a war from which was to issue an atheistic regime (the USSR)—the logical fruit of a civilization that had become desacralized, secularized, rationalized and warped by a philosophical idealism that was bound to produce atheistic materialism. We will go deeper into this issue in the third part of this paper.

Our Plan

The principles thus postulated have a *methodological and general application for all apparitions*. It would seem proper to consider the presentation of the special message of Fatima in terms of the Scriptures—to clarify it, authenticate it, interpret it, and place it in context in relation to the inspired Word of God. We will be able only to skim the surface. It will be an overflight, because a thorough biblical study would require one or more volumes. This presentation will seek to provide a few key correlations between the message of Fatima and the Scriptures, based on the principles already defined.

We will begin with considerations that touch on the experience of the visionaries: sin, repentance, conversion, reparation. That is the *earthly* pole of the message, its praxis side—how it has been lived out by the visionaries. This is much more fundamental than the "theology" of Fatima, because from the theological and ecclesial point of view, the *receptio* of the dogma and the doctrine—the manner in which it is received and lived out—is of capital importance. A dogma is revealed by God as a message of love, to be lived out.

We will then move to the *theological* pole. That which comes from God's messengers—the angel and the Virgin, that which comes from heaven. This theology is essentially theocentric in that the angel and the Virgin appear only in the light of God Himself. It is essentially eschatological, for Fatima is an invitation to heaven, via a shortcut for Francisco and Jacinta, and the long route for Lucia. Like all visionaries, those at Fatima do not fear death. They long for it, having had the benefit of a foretaste of heaven.

We will also emphasize how this heavenly and divine pole is solidified in the heart by the Incarnation: Christ's heart and Mary's heart. This aspect of the heart is very important in the message of Fatima. Since the visionaries receive everything in the light of God, it will be legitimate to say, with St. John Eudes, that these two hearts are but one *(anatomically two,* but since Jesus' heart was formed in Mary, there is a unity of origin and of love: They are *spiritually* and *morally one).* To speak about the heart is one way to understand divine love at the human level of the Word Incarnate, the Christ who lived out divine love in our nature. This shows that the transcendent God is also intimate. He has deigned to speak to man in the language of the heart, and he asks us for prayer and self-surrender from the heart.

Finally, we will place in context the *prophetic* dimension of the message of Fatima, for it is linked to world history. It kindles hope and prepares for the future: the end of war and the conversion of Russia. We will see that this message is apocalyptic and eschatological in nature.

In conclusion, we will seek to place this message in the context of the extension of these three poles: (1) earthly praxis, (2) divine light (heavenly), and (3) historical scope: prophetic and apocalyptic. These are merely three aspects of the same shock wave destined to bring earthly man back to God—man who is constantly bent of following his own animality, systematized by a prideful rationality that substitutes itself for God. Man is a tributary both of original sin (he seeks to be like God by disobeying God (Gen 3: 5–6)) and of the sin of Babel— to reach heaven by human techniques (Gen 11). What man needs is to be led to heaven in this temporal world by personal, graced self-surrender to God and his word. Thus God prophetically involves all those who love Him and love humanity—those who pray and sacrifice themselves for the future of the world in an authentic cooperation with the history of salvation and achieve in themselves the work of Christ for the sake of his body which is the Church (cf. Col 1:24).

THE VARIOUS ASPECTS OF THE MESSAGE OF FATIMA

The Earthly Pole of the Message of Fatima As Experienced and Praxis of Conversion

The message of Fatima is a heavenly vision, which created in the visionaries an intense attraction to God and heaven. But this heavenly message left them with their feet solidly on the ground among their flocks, with their daily obligations, and, in the forefront, with an austere spiritual program to which they dedicated themselves wholeheartedly. This is of primary importance in understanding the message of Fatima. Once again, we cannot separate the message from the manner in which it was lived out by the two little visionaries, who died before they were ten and whose heroic virtue has recently been recognized by the pope.

Francisco Marto, born on June 11, 1908, died on April 4, 1919, at age ten.

Jacinta Marto, born on March 11, 1910, died on February 20, 1920, at age nine.

Lucy, who is today an octogenarian, received the mission of giving testimony through a long life full of sharp turns: her solitary testimony contradicted and criticized, her transfers from one order to another, from Portugal to Spain, and again from Spain to Portugal.

Prayer

Like the message of Lourdes, the message of Fatima is essentially a message of prayer, with emphasis on the rosary. The Virgin appeared with the rosary, whose beads sparkled like pearls against her white dress (JN, p. 73). At each of the six apparitions, the Virgin recommended that the visionaries say the rosary daily. That was her most constant leitmotif.

In the form that we now know, the Rosary is a rather recent devotion. It is the ultimate and remarkable adaptation of a type of vocal prayer, repetitive and meditative, that has been used since the days of St. Dominic. The Dominican Alan de la Roche launched it in 1470 as a type of community prayer for prayer groups. Regarding our theme, *Fatima and Scripture*, two observations will suffice. The 150 Hail Mary's of the Rosary can be seen as a substitute for the 150 Psalms, for the benefit of the poor and illiterate. It is a prayer indeed inspired by the Bible—a popular adaptation of the Divine Office drawn from the Book of Psalms. On another level, the Rosary is especially a *Bible for the poor*, leading to meditation on the mysteries of the Gospel: the joyful mysteries of the infancy (Luke 1 and 2), the sorrowful mysteries of the Passion, where the Virgin was also present, and the glorious mysteries of Resurrection, Ascension, Pentecost (Acts 1 and 2), where the Virgin again participated, extended by two mysteries of the glorification of the Virgin—Assumption and Coronation. These last two mysteries find their biblical sources in Revelations chapter twelve, of which Fatima (like Guadalupe, the Miraculous Medal, Lourdes, etc.) is an echo.

Sin, Sacrifice, Penance

According to the threefold perspective of the theologian Hans

---

1. JN—Dom Claude Jean-Nesmy, *(The Truth of Fatima) La venti de Fatima*, Paris: SOS, 1980.

Urs Von Balthasar in *Esthetic, Dramatic, Theological*, the message of Fatima is less *esthetic* and *theological* than *dramatic*. It is certainly a drama that is lived by the visionaries, interpellated by the very light of God that illuminates for them the horrors of hell and draws them toward heaven, in the footsteps of Christ and of the Virgin herself. This drama is the drama of sin and of sinners, a theme that constantly recurs in the message.

Sinners are the object of a tremendous compassion that comes from above, from heaven. They are reminded of the possiblity of hell, toward which all who turn away from God are racing.

Hell

Hell occupies a prominent place in the message of Fatima. It is presented as the destiny of the free man who rejects God's love by turning back to his own egoism and pride through mortal sin. The visionaries' compassion for those headed toward hell is inspired by Christ and Mary. The mention of hell culminates in a vision that constitutes the first part of the famous three part secret of Fatima (to which Lucia referred in the apparition of July 13, 1917). Having spoken of the conversion of sinners and reparation for sins, Mary Immaculate:

> again opened her hands, as she had done the preceding two months. The reflection from her hands seemed to penetrate the earth's surface, and we saw what looked like an ocean of fire. Plunged into this fire we saw demons and the souls of the damned. They were like transparent embers, black or bronze, with the form of human beings. They floated in that conflagration wafted by the flames that burst forth with clouds of smoke, falling on every side, like sparks that fall from great fires, unrestrained and uncontrolled, amid cries and groans of pain and despair that horrified and made one tremble with fear.

It was the sight of this spectacle that caused me to cry out Oh! Oh! which people said they heard me do.

The demons appeared as horrible and repugnant types of extraordinary and unknown animals. They, too, were transparent, like charred blazing coals.

In the third memoir, Lucy specified: "This vision lasted only a moment, thanks to our good heavenly Mother, who had already promised in the first apparition to take us to heaven. Without that, I believe that we would have died of horror and fear" (L 104; cf. JN 87).

The fourth memoir continues: "You have seen hell, where the souls of lost sinners go. To save them, God wants to establish in the world the devotion to my Immaculate Heart!" (JN p. 87; L 163).[2]

Let us briefly contrast this vision of hell with the Gospel. Are the two in conformity? At Fatima, as in the Gospel, hell is a real place—inhabited by the fallen angels and the souls of the damned. The fires of hell light up the horrible scene, but it is with light unlike the light of God. It is the blazing light of a world that has refused love—a self-combustion of nihilism and despair. Fatima and the Gospel clearly agree that hell is the absence of God and the presence of fire. Those who accuse Fatima of engaging in mythology would have to level the same accusation at the Gospel, Christ frequently described hell in clear and concrete terms:

"Burning oven...Tears and gnashing of teeth" (Mt 13:42; cf. 8:12; 13:50; 22:13; 24:51; 25:30; Lk 13:28).

"Gehenna where the fire is not quenched" (Mk 9:43–48; cf. Mt 5:22).

"For the loss of soul and body" (Mt 10:28) [cf. the parable of the rich man "tormented in this flame" (Lk 16:24)].

---

2. *Lucie raconte Fatima (Lucy Tells about Fatima)*, presented by Dom Claude Jean-Nesmy, Paris: DDB, 1975.

The language of the Gospel (especially in the parable of the rich man is even more polyvalent: "the worm that never dies" (Mk 9:43–48). That is the *scolex*: an insect that attacks living organic matter and is not revealed until its decomposition (2 Mc 9:9; Acts 12:23). It signifies the internal destruction of life for those who chose egoism over life (Is 14:11; 66:24; Mk 9:48).

Hell is not a cruel action external to the Almighty. It is an immanent justice. God has left man free to make his own decisions (Sir 15:14). He can choose love or egoism, God or human pride, the order of God's law or the destructive disorder of vice. It is *sin* that is the source of evil, because this human failing disorganizes and disintegrates a world that was created good. The very choice of sin casts into hell a multitude of people who have refused love.

Hell flows from God's immanent justice on two counts. The sinner deprives himself of love, which he has flouted by violating God's beneficial laws—prerequisites for human integrity and an eternal future. Through sin, man destroys himself. By refusing love, man yields himself to the maggots of his pride and egoism. He ignites in himself this fire which burns him, whereas he had been made for the fire that warms, nourishes, and gives life. Hell is therefore the opposite of the confidence God places in man. God sets man up as a free partner to his love, which He does not impose but rather proposes. He has such a great desire for all to be saved that He became man and gave his life for man's salvation.

God's love multiplies the means to awaken human freedom and elicit a response to his love. God-made-man gave sinners a priority, a sort of preferential option: "I did not come to call the righteous but sinners" (Mt 9:13; Mk 2:17; cf. Lk 15:2, 10). The word *Gospel* (Good News announced to the poor) signifies that priority for the poor. A priority which is without boundary and extends even to sinners.

In anticipation of the third part of this report, let us add that the message of Fatima refers to the other consequences of sin:

the evils, the wars, the persecutions that come from the systematic atheism of the USSR. The message of Fatima is a warning, a fire alarm. It is an invitation to avert evil and hell, but also the war and violence that result from sin—a message that is always timely: "If you do what I tell you, many souls will be saved and there will be peace. The war will end. But if you do not stop offending God, during the reign of Pius XI there will be another one, even worse."

Reparation, Sacrifice: Antidotes to Sin

The message of Fatima places particular emphasis on what the visionaries are to do. They are not only to avoid hell themselves, but to help others avoid it by acts of *reparation and sacrifice*. The penitential lives of the visionaries was not motivated solely by personal fear of hell, nor even by a compelling compassion for sinners, but *first of all* by the concern to console God and the Virgin, to make reparation for the sadness that sin causes them.

To Lucia, who asked, "What would you prefer: to console Our Lord or to convert sinners so that they will not go to hell?" Francisco answered without hesitation:

> I would prefer to console Jesus. Didn't you see how sad Our Lady was [during the apparition of October 13] when she said that men must stop offending Our Lord Who has already been so offended? I would like to console Our Savior AND THEN CONVERT THE SINNERS, SO THAT THEY WILL NO LONGER OFFEND HIM" (L 4th Memoir, p. 138; cf. B 148–149).[3]

And again:

---

3. B—Ferdinand Baumann, S.J. *Fatima et le salut du Monde (Fatima and the Salvation of the World)*, Mulhouse: Salvator, 1953.

I offer that to console Our Lord and Our Lady, and then I offer it for sinners and for the Holy Father (L 139; cf. p. 146).

One day, when Francisco had been fasting for a long time and Lucia in astonishment asked him why, he answered: "I am thinking about *God* who is so saddened by so many sins. If only I were able to make him happy!" (ibid.).

Francisco placed God's happiness ahead of his own, just as Christ placed men's happiness ahead of his own worldly joys. During his illness, the young boy would say, "Yes, I am suffering, but I hope in this way to console the Savior. Soon I will go to heaven. I will console Our Lord and the Blessed Virgin" (B, p. 149). So far beyond egotistic concerns had he progressed that he was going to heaven to *give* some more, without thinking about what he would *receive*.

To please God and to save sinners are not two disparate motives. They are the same. That is God's great desire—to save sinners from hell. That is why He died. Francisco understood this and devoted himself to a life of profound prayer and demanding penance. The children's response to the message lies within the tradition of the great ascetics whose achievements, love and courage stir us and cause us to reflect on the extent to which we have forgotten the cross and sacrifice.

Sacrifice holds a prominent place in the message of Fatima. It is the dominant means of reparation for the conversion of sinners. The theme is repeated with insistence. Thus, during the second apparition of the angel at the peak of the summer of 1916, after the invitation to prayer, the angel added (according to Lucia's recollection):

"Constantly offer prayer and sacrifice to the Most High" (L 4th document, p. 155).

"What are we to sacrifice?"

"All that you can. Offer to God a sacrifice, as an act of reparation for the sins that offend him, and of supplication for the conversion of sinners. Thus you will gain peace for your country. I am its guardian angel, the angel of Portugal. In particular, accept and bear submissively the sufferings which God will send you" (L. 155; JN 65).

Sacrifice is therefore clearly understood as suffering. It is to a strict renunciation that the visionaries pledged themselves. And they lived it without flinching, ardently, like a holocaust. The Virgin returned to the subject in her very first apparition:

> "Do you want to offer yourselves to God to bear all the *sufferings* that he may wish to send you, as an act of reparation for the sins by which he is offended and of supplication for the conversion of sinners?"
> "Yes, we really want to!" repeated the visionaries.
> "You will then have *much to suffer*, but God's grace will comfort you" (last words of the first apparition: L, 4th Memoir, p. 159, cf. JN, p. 75 and 83).

Surely sacrifice is a positive act of returning to God. But it includes a reverse side of renunciation and suffering as a sign and proof of love. The positive aspect was not overlooked in Fatima. The Virgin taught it at the third apparition: "Sacrifice yourselves for sinners and repeat often, whenever you make a sacrifice: Oh Jesus, it is out of love for you, for the conversion of sinners, and in reparation for the sins committed against the Immaculate Heart of Mary" (L, 4th Memoir, p. 162; cf. JN p. 185).

This last message is very important, for it underscores the positive aspect of sacrifice: the love that inspires it, the direction in which it leads, the fruits that result from it. Sacrifice is neither masochism, nor fear, nor concern for achievement. It is love that inspires it. That is the meaning behind the words of Jesus: "There is no greater love than to lay down one's life for those one loves." The paradox of love is that it finds itself by losing itself, and finds happiness by giving itself, according to the profound word of the Gospel: "He who would save his life will lose it. He who loses his life for my sake will find it." Thus the apostle Paul wished to die so he could be with Christ (Phil 1:23; cf. 2 Cor 5:8).

This is in keeping with the very nature of true love, where each party *gives himself or herself* for the happiness of the beloved. Francisco wants to console Jesus, and Jesus will be the happiness of Francisco. Jesus gave his life for us, and he is waiting for us to give our own. Only then will love be perfect and overflowing. This ardent sacrifice of the visionaries, inspired by love, is inseparable from Christ's sacrifice. It is the extension of the Gospel's invitation: "He who wishes to come after me must deny himself, take up his cross and follow me" (Mt 10:39; 16:25; Mk 8:35; 19:24).

At the third apparition of 1916 the angel revealed this link between the sacrifices asked of the visionaries and the sacrifice of Christ Himself. On rising, after having recited several times the prayer "My God, I believe, I adore, I hope, and I love you" (the prayer taught them by the angel in 1916: L, 154), the visionaries "stood up" to see what was happening:

And we saw an angel, holding in his left hand a *chalice* over which was suspended a *Host* from which a few drops of Blood were falling into the chalice. The angel let go of the chalice, which remained suspended in midair. He knelt beside us and had us repeat three times: "Most Holy Trinity, Father, Son, and Holy Spirit, I adore You profoundly and I *offer* You the most precious Body, Blood, Soul and Divinity of Jesus Christ present in all the tabernacles of the world, in reparation for the insults, sacrileges and indifference by which He is offended, and through the infinite merits of his Most Sacred Heart and of the Immaculate Heart of Mary, I beg You for the conversion of sinners (L, p. 156, cf. JN p. 67)."

There then followed the communion of the visionaries. Lucia received the Sacred Host and Jacinta and Francisco were given the Precious Blood to drink. Communion was accompanied by these words:

> Take and drink the Body and the Blood of Jesus Christ, horribly insulted by ungrateful men. Make reparation for their crimes and console your God (L, p. 156 and JN p. 67).

The language here is dramatic. It is a drama of pure love: the love of God, wounded by men and unappreciated by men.

Here again, it is Francisco who will heroically go the furthest in reparation. He deprives himself of liquid in a very hot climate. Francisco was called to an exceptional level of sacrifice to recall and compensate for the forgetfulness by so many Christians of sacrifice. These very excesses lie in the wake of the excess of love God has for us. For the love that drove Jesus to the Cross is folly to human wisdom. These "excesses" of the children are meant to redress the faults committed here below by the opposite extremes. To straighten a bent shaft, it must be twisted in the opposite direction. The world had abandoned itself to its pleasures and desires in line with the principles of Freud, who was then at the height of his career. It was important at that moment in history—in our moment of history—to recall the gospel teaching on sacrifice and the central message of the Gospel: *Christ redeemed men by his suffering and his death*. The Son of God, the Almighty Creator of the universe, chose to ransom the world through the bloody sacrifice of his body on the altar of the cross. He could have avoided this, but He freely accepted it as the greatest proof of love.

Christ's sacrifice was in obedience (Heb 3:7–8) to an internal law that in the final analysis was the law of love (Jn 14:31; 15:13). We are called to follow the austere way of Christ (Jn 15:20; Mt 10:24), which is a way of love. The message of Fatima reminds us of this way, a way that is as forgotten as it is important. Love is a gift. It is conveyed by forgetting oneself. It requires discipline, asceticism, sacrifice: a loss that leads to the finding of self by the reciprocal gift of those we love (Mk 10:30). It is possible to make sacrifices for all the ills and sufferings that assail us in this world. But it is also possible, like the visionaries of Fatima, to cultivate the practice of voluntary sacrifices offered out of love for God. It is important to discern which sacrifices contribute to the achievement of love, for the *end result* of sacrifice is not destruction and suffering, but attainment.

That is the profound meaning of Christ's word: "If anyone wants to be a follower of mine, let him renounce himself" (Lk 9:23). And the Apostle Paul, from the depth of his own experience, which was analogous to that of the visionaries of Fatima, said: "In my own body I do what I can to make up all that is still to be undergone by Christ for the sake of his body, the Church" (Col 1:24).

The children of Fatima are engaged in the realization of the message—like the poor, without riches, without culture, without teaching (the truly poor). Like the widow in the Gospel (Mt 12: 41–43), they have given all they have. They have sacrificed even the essentials. With their whole being, they have met the greatest proof of love given by Christ (Jn 15:13). The Virgin restrained their mortification along the way. She was quick to urge them to give up the painful practice of wearing a thick rope around their waists, which prevented them from sleeping. She asked them to take the rope off at night. They needed their sleep for their psychic integrity, necessary in the very exercise of their love. This moderating intervention makes a great deal of sense.

Instruments of penance (which constituted a veritable arsenal at the dawn of this century: hairshirts, scourges, iron bracelets, etc.) are now but museum pieces. But the post-conciliar abolition of these implements should not cause us to forget the essential place of sacrifice in the Christian life. Reason itself invites us today to choose sacrifices that are not self-destructive but give the body greater strength and health for the service of God and his people.

For example, fasting, which had been poorly understood and

was gradually disappearing, has witnessed an unprecedented resurgence at the end of the decade of the eighties. Fasting requires some effort. It runs counter to the pull of desire. But if it is poorly understood, it purifies, strengthens, and promotes the health of the body for God's service. It provides a person with the mastery of his instincts, both alimentary and sexual. It represents a return to the Gospel (Mt 6:16–18), where we are invited to cast out demons "by prayer and fasting" (Mt 17:21). While Christ suspended fasting, which had been warped by the Pharisees, during the "visit of the Spouse"—as He called his time on earth (Mk 2:19—we see in Acts 6:5, 11:27 and 13: 2–3 as well as in 2 Cor 11:27 that the early Christians were quick to reinstate fasting. It is in this sense of mortifying useless or harmful desires that we must reorient penance, which was admirable although not imitable in every detail in the lives of the visionaries of Fatima.

Consecration

The children of Fatima vigorously faced the difficult aspect of sacrifice: the wall of suffering. For them, sacrifice was an essentially positive act, the fearless rush of love toward God leading to a consecration of the whole being.

The message of Fatima urged consecration in a world that was becoming increasingly desacralized, secularized, atheistic and materialistic. The message of the Virgin on this subject is found at the heart of the second secret of Fatima. "To prevent" the Second World War and its resulting "famine" and "persecution," the Virgin declares:

> I will come to ask for the consecration of Russia to my Immaculate Heart and the communion of reparation on the first Saturday of each month. If my request is heard, Russia will be converted and there will be peace.... The Holy Father will consecrate Russia to me, and she will

be converted, and thus the world will enjoy a time of peace.
(L, 3rd Memoir, p. 105).

The Fourth Memoir added at this point: "Portugal will always preserve the dogma of faith" (there follow three suspension points marking the place of the third secret of Fatima—the one that has not been revealed to this day: L, 163–164).

It seems to me that no trace of this consecration can be found in the lives of Francisco and Jacinta. It is as though the message of consecration had found its explanation only later, in the second phase of the Fatima revelations made to Lucia. This is not the place to study that problem. Let us merely place this message in its historical context.

In Scriptures, Christians are called "saints," consecrated to God by water and the Holy Spirit in Baptism. The Apostle Paul does not hesitate to call Christians "saints' and to consider the presence of a sinner among them abnormal and serious, existing only by way of exception. In later times, including our own day, Christians have always been consecrated by Baptism, but it has often been an inoperative consecration. The baptismal birth results in too many stillborns, in whom the faith does not live. The situation has become worse in modern times. The world has continued to become more and more secularized. This process began with the Renaissance: that cultural wave, begun in the fifteenth century, turned Christians away from Christian sources and back to pagan ones. Then came the spreading "conversion" to scientific rationalism, a further turning away from God that led from the anticlerical theism of the philosophers of the enlightenment to the atheism of the nineteenth century and that tolled the knell of the so-called "death of God" movement. That century was marked by the birth of Marxism (decade of the 1840s), whose effective reign began in 1917, the year of Fatima.

Very early, in the fervent Spain of the seventeenth century, the paganization of the world prompted a great movement of consecration as reparation for this desacralization. In the midst of the disintegration of Christianity, many Christians came to understand the necessity of an effective consecration, under the auspices of the Virgin to whom God had confided Himself for his humanization and to whom He confided us for our divinization (Jn 19: 25-27). A creature consecrated by excellence, and the abode of Christ's consecration, she has an unrivaled mission for the consecration of the world and of each of the children of men. That is what was perceived in the Spanish movement of consecration led by Bartholomew of Los Rios. Then came the representatives of the French School: from Berulle to Grignon de Montfort to so many others in the nineteenth and twentieth centuries including St. Maximilian Kolbe. All these movements have promoted a personal consecration that actualizes and realizes the consecration of Baptism. They were well inspired to place everything in the hands of the Virgin Mary, the Mother of Christ's disciples.

The message of Fatima amplifies this movement of consecration. Recent popes (Pius XII, Paul VI, and John Paul II) have on eight occasions renewed, under diverse forms (which are still being discussed), the consecration of the world—paying very special attention to the consecration of Russia.

Here, biblical hermeneutics must point out that the language of Fatima short-circuits the theocentricism that is essential to consecrations. Just as one cannot adore a creature (that would be idolatry), one cannot offer a sacrifice or consecrate oneself to a creature. Consecration to Christ is fully legitimate because He is God-made-man. But to speak of consecration to the Immaculate Heart of Mary, one must change the authentic and full meaning of the word consecration.

For the sake of theological exactness and ecumenism (which finds this apparent idolatry scandalous), it would be good to explain and even adapt this language, as has been effectively done by certain contemporary theologians—for example S. de Fiores and D. Bertetto in Italy, and Cardinal Sin in the Philippines. Nothing is lost by understanding this consecration to the Immaculate Heart of Mary as a consecration to God, for

God alone can consecrate us and divinize us. That understanding neither eliminates nor diminishes the role of Mary, for one can and should *give oneself* and *abandon oneself* to her, as God did at the Incarnation. It is good to *place oneself without restriction* in the hands of Mary our Mother, so that she can dispose us to this consecration to God and by God, in which she participates by her unique communion with God. It is in this sense that we should resolve the difficulties certain theologians have with the consecration asked for at Fatima. In this way we will also avoid useless ecumenical clashes.

So much for the earthly and anthropological pole of the message: conversion (fundamentally identical to consecration since it consists in turning completely toward God), reparation, asceticism, suffering, sacrifice—this is the most concrete and evident part of the message. But the impetus and motivation for conversion and reparation come from above. Now we must consider the heavenly pole of the message.

2. The Heavenly Pole of the Message of Fatima. The Theocentricism of Fatima

Love

The primary motivation of the visionaries is love. This word appeared at the very outset, in the angel's message as reported by Lucia, (the prayer revealed during the first apparition of the angel in the spring of 1916) (L, 154, 4th Memoir; cf. JN 67): "My God, I love you. . . . I ask your pardon . . . for all those who do not love you."

And during the second apparition of the Virgin: "Jacinta and Francisco, I will soon take them. . . . But you, you will remain here for some time. Jesus wants to use you to make me known and *loved*. He wants to establish throughout the world devotion to my Immaculate Heart" (Fourth Memoir, L, 161; JN p. 81).

At the third apparition, the Virgin asked: "Sacrifice yourselves for sinners, and say often, especially each time you make a sacrifice: Oh Jesus, it is *for love you*, for the conversion of sinners and in reparation for the sins committed against the Immaculate Heart of Mary" (Fourth Memoir, L, 162; cf. JN 85).

Love is the spring, the impetus for all the rest, including sacrifice and penance, with the priority definitely placed on love. However strong was the fear of hell, it was secondary in terms of this motivation of love. And this motivation was doubly entwined in the desire for heaven, that is for God Himself who is love. For God is Love (Jn 4:8 and 16) and He calls us to share his life. That is one of the most constant themes of the Gospel.

The desire for heaven was granted to the visionaries in the perception of God as light, which we must now examine. This theme of God as light is the essence of the message received by the visionaries. The perception, the attraction of the love of God was their primary focus.

The Mediators

They had been brought to this focus by means of a double mediation. The first was through the mediation of the angel, at the time of the two apparitions of April and October 1915, followed by the three visions in the spring, summer, and autumn of 1916.

The other mediation by which the visionaries had a more direct access to the experience of God was that of the Virgin Mary.

This first mediation recalls the biblical theology of angels. Of course, an entire volume could easily be devoted to the truth of angels and their role in the mystery of salvation (cf. Mt 8:10, Heb 1:14, Rev 5:11–12). Let us put in context the impact of the scriptural teaching on angels.

Modern theology is experiencing a renewed interest in angels. There is now a tendency to return to them. New books are being published on this topic. As a precursor to this trend, the great poet Patrice de la Tour du Pin had a great devotion to angels, and he strongly and poetically defended them during the French liturgical renewal which he had been called upon to help.

On a basic level, divine creation is infinitely generous. The earth and its variety of species are a manifestation of this incredible generosity. (Our pillaging of the planet unfortunately causes the disappearance of various species each year.) In the hierarchy of God's creatures, there is a place for the spiritual creatures spoken of in the Bible and properly situated in the theology of Thomas Aquinas. These superior brothers, pure spirits, provide a link between the transcendent God and us, rational animals and therefore inferior brothers, but infinitely elevated by the privilege of the Incarnation and also by the power which God gives to man (but not to angels) to engender his own species. With this as a starting point, a whole theology of angels could be developed.

It can also be developed by considering Jesus' experience of angelic help. Following the Lord many Christians throughout the ages have experienced the direct help and guidance of the angels. Consequently, devotion to the angels has developed in the Church—especially devotion to Michael, the Prince of the Angels, and to the Guardian Angels. A consideration of angels must include this live experience.

As for the Angel of Portugal, he has his roots in biblical tradition. According to Dt 32:8, the Most High fixed the number of nations according to "the number of the sons of God," that is, the angels, but He reserved Israel, his chosen people, for himself personally (Dt 32:8; cf. 7:6 and Dn 10:13, where the prince of Persia appears as one of the protector angels of nations inimical to Israel; cf. Eccl 17 in the Septuagint version).

Light

These two mediators, the angel and the Virgin Mary, appear in the divine light. The visionaries describe the angel in terms of light. Regarding the apparitions of 1915, Lucia described the angel as follows:

I saw, above the trees of the valley that stretched below us, gliding like a cloud whiter than snow, something transparent that had a human form (L, Fourth Memoir, 153; JN 58 says, based on other documents, "A statue of snow which the sun's rays seemed to render transparent").

For the first apparition of 1916 (spring), she wrote:

A light whiter than snow, which had the form of a young man, a transparent light, more brilliant than crystal, laced by the sun's rays. As the apparition came closer, we were better able to distinguish its traits (L, p. 154; JN 60 specifies, based on other documents, "the same face as in 1915, a young man fourteen or fifteen years old, whiter than snow, whom the sun rendered transparent like a remarkably beautiful crystal").

The reference to the brightness of snow recalls the Transfiguration in the Gospel, in a variant of Mt 17:2: "His clothing became white as snow," (the alternate text says "as light"). And the robe of the angel at the Resurrection "was white as snow," according to Mt 28:3.

The visionaries were to summarize their impressions in an answer to a question from Canon Barthas:
"What did he look like?"

"Erade Luz, He looked like light...."
But it was an "unknown light," said Lucia regarding the third apparition (JN, p. 67).

The light of the angel was preceded by what Lucia sometimes called *relampago—a lightning*. She was to explain that it was not violent lightning, like that accompanied by thunder. The appearance of the angel is accompanied, from the very first apparition, with the words: "Do not fear," a classical greeting in biblical apparitions (notably Lk 1:13 and 30; 2:10; 5:10). There is also an invitation to prayer (1, 154).

Similarly, the Lady appears more brilliant than the sun, like a crystal... laced with the rays of the sun (JN pp. 72 and 73). These terms blend with the vision of *Revelation*, where the Virgin appears "clothed with the sun" (Rv 12:1). And Tradition identifies the sun with Christ, the "Sun of Justice," in this passage of Rv 1:16: "His face was like the sun shining with all its force."

The light of Our Lady shines, radiates and conquers the visionaries. The beads of their rosaries shine like pearls. They are dazzled by this light they can barely stand. The light reaches their eyes but also their hearts, for it is the light of a presence.

God is Light

At the end of the first apparition (as we have already noted), the Virgin opens her hands and communicates:

> by a reflection emanating from them, a light so intimate that, penetrating our heart to the depths of our soul, she enabled us to see ourselves in God, **God Who was that light** (Fourth Memoir, L 160; JN 75: first apparition).

The light that enveloped the Virgin was God Himself, said Lucia in a striking summary. For it was not a question of a tangible light, but of a mysterious light that touched the heart and the soul and made contact with God Himself. Hence this immediate reaction:

> We fell on our knees and repeated from the bottom of our heart: O Most Holy Trinity, I adore you! My God, my God, I love you in the Blessed Sacrament (L, 160; JN, p.75).

And Francisco declared:

> It was a great joy for me to see the angel, but my joy was even greater when I saw Our Lady. But what filled me

with the greatest joy of all was **to see God in this light which Our Lady was directing into our hearts** (B, p. 147).

Francisco here reveals his deepest experience. It coincides with the biblical experience where God is characterized by light. Before anything else, He created light (Gen 1:3). It is the raiment with which he is clothed (Ps 104:2). When He appears "his brightness is like the day, rays flash from his hands" (Hb 3:4). "The heavenly vault on which rests his throne is as sparkling as crystal" (Ex 24:10; Ez 1:22). He is Himself light: "Wisdom is a reflection of eternal light... more beautiful than the sun" (Wis 7:26 and 29). The following verses from John's prologue state it more specifically: "In the beginning was the Word and the Word was God.... The Word was the true light that enlightens all men" (Jn 1:1 and 9). These words serve as the perfect foundation for the striking statement of little Francisco, dated October 13, which we have just quoted.

It is therefore the light of God which, through Our Lady who was shining with that light, penetrated the hearts and lives of the visionaries in a definite way, and then came to enlighten, by contrast, hell itself: in other words, the opposite of love, the anti-love, the despair of love refused by those who elect to refuse it.

The vision of God determines, by an "interior impulse," the prostration of the visionaries and adoration "from the bottom of the heart," with this prayer:

O Most Holy Trinity, I adore you! My God, my God, I love you in the Most Blessed Sacrament (L, 160).

The Heart

Another symbol, another filtering of the light, more humble, more familiar, is the heart.

For God is both *transcendent* and *familiar*. These two characteristics are not in opposition. They complement one another. God is all the more familiar because He is transcendent. He is all the more intimate with us because his transcendence allows Him to be our Creator and to create even our freedom. This He gives us in full autonomy, by making each created person a full partner, master of his own destiny, capable of loving, but also of refusing his love.

The revelations to St. Margaret Mary of the Sacred Heart manifest this intimacy, this familiarity, and this love of Christ, according to the symbol of the heart still used daily even in our times. Some theologians call it archaic and outdated in this age of heart surgery, but it is seen everywhere in popular slogans: I [heart] New Year, I [heart] my cat, we [heart] our clients, etc.

The heart of Jesus is not separated from the heart of Mary, his Sacred Heart was formed by her. She achieved with Him the most perfect communion. Thus the angel taught the following prayer to the visionaries at the third apparition of 1916:

> Through the infinite merits of the Blessed Heart [of Christ] and of the Immaculate Heart of Mary, I ask you for the conversion of the poor sinners (Fourth Memoir, L., 456; JN p. 67).

These two hearts form but one, according to St. John Eudes, who speaks in the singular about the heart of Jesus and Mary. This unity appeared in the message of Fatima.

It assumed a rather paradoxical nature when the Virgin said (at the apparition of Pontevedra on December 10, 1925): "My daughter, see my heart surrounded with thorns which ungrateful people sink into it at every moment by their blasphemies and their ingratitude." There followed the request for people to go to communion on the first Saturday of five consecutive months (JN, p. 213).

Some people are surprised that the Virgin spoke of her heart, rather than send people back to the Heart of Christ. And, in that same apparition, the Child Jesus spoke in like manner:

> Have compassion on the heart of your very Holy

Mother, covered with thorns, which ungrateful men sink into it at every moment, while there is no one to make an act of reparation to pull them out (JN, p. 213).

This placing of the Virgin in the forefront clashes with the theocentrism that we have been rigidly applying. The explanation may lie in that perfect communion, that unity of the two hearts, and in Christ's plan to manifest the Virgin, his mother, to whom He confided such an important role in the incarnation and to whom He wants to grant an important role in the end times. But the topic remains one of the most delicate and difficult points for the interpretation of Fatima.

The heart is a symbol that turns off the modern intellectual. For him, the heart is just an organ like the other organs, a pump that takes care of circulating the blood and that can be repaired by cardiac surgery.

The revelation of the Heart of Christ occurred at the outset of the rationalist era, as a compensation and a remedy for its abstraction, against which our culture is finally beginning to react today. This revelation involves a return to the Bible, where the heart has a definite place—not so much as an organ, but as the inner being, as John Paul II summarized it so well in his homily at the Gemelli Hospital (June 24, 1984). The heart is, the Holy Father noted:

> That essential center of the personality in which man stands before God like a totality of body and soul, like the *I* thinking, wanting, loving, like the center in which the memory of the past opens toward the future.

The playing down of the heart and its return to prominence, through private revelations that have occurred since St. Margaret Mary, help explain the core of cultural problems.

Our Western culture—that of the Greeks as well as the Latins—seems allergic to the heart, as D. Fernandez so sensibly put it in *Ephemerides Mariologicae* 37 (1987, p. 87). The

Bible (from a semitic culture) uses the word "heart" (*leb* or *lebad*) 853 times in the Old Testament and 159 times in the New Testament, which comes down to us from the Greek, and it is quite possible that the word "heart" was removed in the Greek translation of the account of the piercing of the Crucified (Jn 19:34), which refers instead to the *side* of Christ. In any case, the word "heart" is rare among the Fathers. They prefer the world "spirit," for Greek philosophy situates man's rational principle in his head rather than in his heart, in his intelligence rather than his sensibility. Scholastic philosophy, which raised the value of abstraction and somehow devalued symbols, has favored this relegation. But God no doubt has a heart, for He has reacted through private revelations.

Despite the Greek repugnance to the use of the word, the New Testament has preserved the foundation for the theology of the heart of Jesus and Mary: "I am meek and humble of heart," said Jesus in Mt 11:29. He often referred to the heart: "Blessed are the pure of heart, for they shall see God" (Mt 5:8); "Whoever looks covetously upon a woman has already committed adultery with her in his heart" (Mt 5:28); "Where your treasure is, there also will your heart be" (Mt 6:21); and others.

And Luke's Gospel twice repeats, with variants that are not worth detailing here: "Mary preserved [and pondered: *symballousa* in 2:19] these words-and-events in her heart" (Lk 2:19 and 51).

The piercing of Jesus' side is also a transfixion of his heart, in view of the water and the blood that flowed from it (Jn 19:30).

Simeon's prophecy: "A sword will pierce your soul" (*psyche*: Lk 2:35) obviously concerns the heart, and that is probably the word used in the original semitic language, but changed in the Greek translation. In the Septuagint, the word "heart" is repeatedly translated by *psyche*: 2 Chr 7:11; 9:1; 15:15; 31:21; Ps 68:20, 32; Is 7:2, 4; 10:7; Jer 4:19). A good case can be made therefore, that the word "heart" was similarly the original semitic word used in the event recounted in Lk 2:35.

As with St. Margaret Mary, the heart signifies not only *love*, but *sensibility*—the pain of *a heart wounded* by sin (text already quoted from the apparition at Pontevedra, December 10, 1925, JN p. 213). The heart of Mary is "surrounded by thorns" with which sinners are "constantly piercing" it.

We find here again the theme of suffering in heaven, which is to be undertsood from two perspectives:

—The suffering of Christ in his passion are contemporaneous with his eternal *I*, which encompasses at every moment every instant of time. His eternal *I* has taken on, once for all, the sufferings caused by the sins of the world. They are over with temporally in his humanity, but remain an eternal sign of his love and his redemption.

—Christ takes up, along with his personal sufferings, the compassion of his mother; for it is not without a profound plan that He invited her to take part in such an atrocious test. That also remains in the synchronous eternity.

The place of the heart in the message of Fatima consists in returning to the important place the heart has in the Bible, and to the more abrupt anthropomorphisms of the Old Testament regarding God's anger and the human sentiments that are ascribed to him to help understand that terrible affront that sin is.

Prophetic Pole of the Message of Fatima: An Apocalyptic and Eschatological Message

A third dimension of the message of Fatima (after its human earthly dimension and its divine heavenly dimension) is its prophetic one.

In contrast to the messages of Lourdes and of the Miraculous Medal, the message of Fatima pertains to specific current events, to history, and to the future of the world. It has an apocalyptic message in the sense of the word *apocalypsis*, which means unveiling, revelation. The literary genre of revelation, which is both pre-biblical and biblical, deals more precisely with the revelation of secrets concerning the end times and the course of history. That is certainly the case with the message of Fatima, which falls to some degree in the wake of the genre illustrated by the Bible, from the *apocalypse of Isaiah* (24–27) to the final book of the New Testament. The language of Fatima presents apocalyptic traits: dramatic visions of hell, but also of the future. The message refers to current events in the world and to its future in two very concrete ways.

The War

Second secret of Fatima contains predictions relative to the First World War, in which Portugal became embroiled on March 9, 1916, and to the threat of the Second World War, which indeed came to pass.

This echoes the apocalyptic discourse of Christ in the Gospel. He spoke of "wars" and "rumors of wars" (Mt 24:6). The message of Fatima speaks of war in terms of hope, but a hope that is dependent on commitment to prayer, conversion and consecration on the part of mankind.

The Conversion of Russia

As the Blessed Virgin was appearing at Fatima, the Bolshevik revolution installed the reign of atheism in the largest country of the world. This organized, militant atheism was to extend to more than a third of the planet. It was the outcome and the homogeneous fruit of the secular, rationalist civilization that had been steadily "progressing," ever since the Renaissance. It bears witness to a return to paganism, as we noted above.

The atheistic revolution even uses biblical language, which it redefined. Marx was a secular prophet, a prophet of atheism. Intuitively (and not systematically, as Bultmann, Marx sought to demythologize biblical themes, which he retranslated into a purely human, secular language. In it Communism is defined according to a formula literally lifted from the Acts of the Apostles: "To each according to his needs" (Acts 2:45 and 4:35). Such is the eschatological horizon of Marxism, which is still in its first stage: *To each according to his work*. Therein, the kingdom of God becomes the kingdom of the proletariat.

The phrase "blessed are the poor" in the Gospel proclaimed the interior triumph of victorious charity. For Marx this notion merely announces a violent revolution against and smashing revenge on the affluent, who are stripped of their riches and power.

Marx's revolution is quite different from Mary's revolution in her prophetic hymn: the *Magnificat*. The word "revolution" no doubt applies to both cases, for there certainly is an upheavel, a disruption involved: what seemed to be on the top is cast down, and what was on the bottom is exalted.

God has confounded the proud with the very thoughts of their hearts: "He has pulled down princes from their thrones and exalted the lowly. The hungry he has filled with good things, the rich sent empty away" (Lk 1:52–53). But the *Magnificat* is a revolution of God, not of men. It is a revolution of love, not of violence. It is not a question of eliminating the rich, but of promoting them to the dignity of the poor.

To this secular apocalypse of Communism, Our Lady of Fatima counters with an apocalyptic conversion of Russia that will lead to world peace and put an end to persecution—but at the cost of profound repentance, prayer, and consecration.

Finally, the message of Fatima announces the triumph of the Immaculate Heart. It will occur through reparation for sin and through sacrifice, as we have seen. Mary, Christ and God will be recognized and loved.

It is difficult to say to what extent this apocalyptic promise for the future is an earthly promise and to what extent it refers to the eschatological triumph of the Immaculate Heart of Mary in the kingdom fully established by Christ after his Second Coming. No doubt it has an earthly dimension. And, despite the fanaticism against popes who allegedly did not do what the Virgin demanded and are therefore thought to be responsible for the misfortunes of the times, one can perceive in the USSR clear signs and precursors of the predicted conversion. There have been spontaneous conversions in the third generation reared under the iron rod of atheism. *Glasnost* and *Perestroika* have engendered hope among the heroic Christians of that country.

But beyond that perspective, which should encourage our prayer and our consecration, the message of Fatima is oriented toward the final eschatology, toward "the new heavens and the new earth," toward the God of light and the God of love, who will become God of all in all.

CONCLUSION

The profound meaning of Fatima, the key to the three aspects we have examined in turn, is, therefore, the God of light who enlightens us, the God of love who mercifully warns us through his mother and mobilizes us, so that the history of mankind will truly become the history of salvation.

Thus it will be, according to the Bible, that creation will return to its senses. Everything comes from God, for the world has been created by love, it has been created for love, for eternal life. This wondrous love, dramatically wounded by sin, is what the message of Fatima is inviting us to reestablish by giving proper place to penance, suffering, sacrifice. The price Jesus paid we must pay with Him, to reestablish the reign of love with a victory of reconciliation. Faced with the horrors of sin and hell, Fatima is a message of hope and victory. It restores with a sense of urgency the teaching of Scripture: God wills that "all men be saved" (1 Tm 2:4). That implies a commitment to a love that gives all, sacrifices all, consecrates all.

Mary's Option for the Poor

Rev. Bertrand de Margerie, S.J.

The most famous of Fatima pilgrims, Pope John Paul II, is also a passionate advocate of Mary's preferential love for the poor and the humble. In his encyclical letter on the Mother of the Redeemer, the Vicar of Christ states: "We cannot separate the truth about God who saves from the manifestation of his preference for the poor and for the humble, sung in the *Magnificat*" (MR, No. 37). Nor did Mary separate them during her self-manifestation at Fatima in favor of the poor in faith, the atheists of Soviet Russia.

Our Hispanic brothers and sisters are numerous in the United States of today. They often belong to the world of the poor and of the humble. They are the preferred ones of Mary. Following the footsteps of some Latin American theologians of today, let us dispose ourselves to help them more, particularly on a religious level, through the contemplation of Mary's life and compassion, in the context of her Assumption and Eucharistic intercession.

In harmony with the whole of Catholic tradition, we intend to develop in this way our fundamental thought: Mary is the sign and sacrament of the motherly mercy of God towards the poor, of the tenderness of God who defends and loves the poor.

She is the Mother of God in the concrete form that God has given her motherhood: inside a small, despised people—the people of Israel—seemingly marginalized and powerless in the history of the world.

When Mary receives the message of the angel announcing the Incarnation of the Son of God, she is conscious of her solidarity with the salvific history of the people of Israel. Her faith in the divine message is linked with a total self-gift to the God of the promises, to the God who exalts the humble. She collaborates with her Son and God in his mission of spiritual and temporal liberation, till the cross.

For this reason, Mary experiences with Jesus poverty, suffering, flight and exile. The Gospel accounts of her humiliation in Bethlehem, of her persecution by Herod, of her exile in Egypt and of her suffering at Calvary are so many signs of her faithfulness to the commitment accepted at the time of the Annunciation. As John Paul II points out (MR 16), the words of Simeon ("Your son is destined to be a sign of contradiction and a sword will pierce your heart too") constitute a second Annunciation, revealing to Mary that her life would be full of suffering at the side of the suffering Savior, and her motherhood would be obscure and painful.

At the foot of the cross, Mary sees her Son tortured and publicly executed as a criminal. She remains faithful to the cause of Jesus, fully participating in the fidelity of Jesus to his own mission.

Mary remains silent at the foot of the cross. Full of compassion even for the murderers of her only Son, she is temporally powerless, spiritually powerful. She offers the death of Jesus for the humble and humiliated men and women of all times, in reparation of all our sins of pride, for the eternal salvation of all.

In the person of the Sorrowful Mother, in her pierced Heart, we see millions of humble and poor Hispanics in Latin America and here. They experience an unjust misery, as several popes have said. They accept and frequently offer their suffering in a loving and prayerful silence. Mary teaches us the power of compassion in love. More than the loud protests which are sometimes necessary, the silent offerings of the humble convert and save the proud and the rich.

The *fiat* of Mary to the God of the Poor prolongs itself in her *yes* to the sacrifice and death of Jesus, till Easter and beyond. The presence of Mary at Pentecost is her *yes* to the Church as community entrusted with the mission of pursuing the task of Jesus, in poverty, weakness and persecution.

The Assumption of the Heart of Mary is a participation in the glorious victory of the Resurrection of Jesus, the triumph of God's justice over human injustice. She who had given birth to the Son of God near a manger, she whose Heart had been transpierced by a sword of sorrows, she who suffered with the Apostolic Church the first persecutions, has been, after a humble and unknown death, assumed in soul and body to the glory of Heaven, to the face to face vision of her Son. She now sees what she had so perfectly believed: the beautiful divinity of Jesus, his infinite and eternal mercy for us.

The Assumption is the mysterious culmination of the mysterious preference of God for the little ones of this world: a sign of hope for all the poor and for all those who feel solidarity with the humble. The Resurrection of Jesus and the Assumption of Mary show us that the executioners are vanquished by their victims. It is the confirmation of the ways of Mary, of the ways of God, so manifest in the cases of Francisco and Jacinta, both so poor.

We are now able to understand better why the Church of Rome and also the separated churches of the East never celebrate Holy Mass without mentioning the name of Mary. It is as if the Church wanted, ever since the fourth century, to make it plain that she can never celebrate the Memorial of the Son without exalting the memory of his Mother, without having recourse to her intercession. The Church knows and believes that she owes the sacrificial flesh and the victorious death of Jesus to the free and renewed consent of Mary. How could we forget her tears and her compassion as we offer the Blood of her Son?

The Church also knows and believes that the intercession of Mary, as Mother of God, uniquely associated with Christ in the work of our Redemption, is the most powerful, immediately after the prayer of her Son, our Mediator. How could she not have recourse to such an intercession when the Mediatorial Act is being renewed?

Such remembrances might enable us to help our Hispanic brethren, assaulted by anti-Catholic sects, to remain firm in the profession and practice of the Catholic Faith.

We are grateful to so many of our Hispanic brethren for their example of gratitude to the Sorrowful Mother. Their love of Mary helps us to understand better the presence, the active presence of the Mother of Jesus in each of our Masses.

Each time that we receive Holy Communion—and would that it might be every day, like Mary in the Church of Jerusalem (Acts 2: 42–46)—Mary adores her Son in us, offers again each time her past expiation, in Christ, for our prideful neglect of the poor and of her Son in the poor, thanks him each time in our name and begs him each time ardently to make us share in her option for the poor and for the humble. As her Son renews in each Mass his sacrifice on Calvary, so does she, in the glory of her Assumption, renew in our favor, in favor of all the humble, members of the humble Church, her interior activity of adoration, thanksgiving, reparation and supplication at the foot of the Cross and in the Eucharistic celebrations of the Church of Jerusalem, her beloved daughter.

Most particularly, Mary repeats, in favor of all the sacramentally poor, in favor of all those who, without a serious reason, neglect the pressing invitation of the Church to daily participation in the Holy Eucharist, many repeat the prayer that her Son taught us: "Give us this day our daily bread—both the corporeal bread of time and the spiritual bread of Eternal Life, the daily bread of a daily increased preferential love for the poor and the humble of this world of misery, of violence, and of death.

Virgin Mary, our Mother and Sister, we thank you for having accepted, for the sake of our salvation, to suffer poverty, calumnies, flight, exile.

We proclaim your prayerful power over the powerful and the rich. Without forgetting that each one of us is in some way rich and powerful, we beg you to convert the rich and the powerful to a loving option for the human rights of the poor and of the humble, especially for those who are such among our Hispanic brethren.

Questions from the Audience and Responses from the Speakers' Panel

The speakers' panel consists of Rev. Frederick L. Miller; Rev. Eamon R. Carroll, O.Carm.; Rev. Bertrand de Margerie, S. J., and Rev. John De Marchi, I.M.C.

If the Eucharist distributed to the children by the angel was obtained from a tabernacle, can we assume that the chalice was also from a tabernacle, and if so, why was it not missed?

Fr. Eamon R. Carroll:

According to the studies I have read on apparitions, visions, revelations, and prophecies, the things that are observed by the visionaries (in this case the children of Fatima) are not objects that are capable of being photographed and, apparently in most recorded cases, even of being touched. The nature of the visionaries experience is extremely mysterious. It is not a question of hallucinations—there is some extrinsic supernatural cause that has brought about this experience on their part.

So, if an angel appears in bodily form (as was the case), we do know from our faith that angels are not bodily people. But how can a mere human being on this side of the divide appreciate the message of such a messenger without the messenger appearing in human form? The same mysterious aspect is attached to the presence of Our Lady, her Son, St. John, St. Joseph, and any holy person who has appeared in these authentic appartions and revelations. We do know it is part of our faith that the Risen Christ is in the glory of heaven, in human body and spirit, as well, of course, as in divinity. We know that the Mother of Jesus is present there in the fullness of her personality, which includes her body as well as her human soul.

What the answer would be to the difficult question just asked simply eludes us. We do not know that any tabernacle was empty of a chalice holding the blood of Christ during the appearance that was given to the children.

Did the pope consecrate Russia specifically to the Immaculate Heart of Mary—has the request of Mary been fulfilled?

Fr. Frederick L. Miller:

Pope Pius XII did consecrate Russia by name to the Immaculate Heart of Mary. That consecration was renewed by Pope Paul VI one time on the very floor of the Second Vatican Council in the presence of all the Catholic bishops. It was renewed again by Paul VI and then twice by Pope John Paul II.

The Bishop of Fatima was asked this very question. I was there at Fatima at a meeting in April 1989, when Bishop Amaral was presented with the question: "Did the pope consecrate Russia by name—did he do it properly?" The bishop responded that it is the business of the Holy Father. The Holy Father is the head of the Church and he has responsibility for the Church. He has spoken personally on at least two occasions with Sister Lucia. He has a tremendous love and devotion to the Mother of God. After he was shot in 1981 (he almost died because the bullet had been dipped in some kind of poisonous solution) there was a terrible infection, and during that long and difficult recuperation, he had someone bring into the hospital room all of the records of the Fatima apparitions, which he then reviewed. That is why a year later he went back to Fatima, on May 13, 1982, to thank Mary for saving his life. At that time he renewed the consecration. He consecrated the Church again with Christ's consecration of Himself for the sanctification of the world. It's really the consecration of the Church as the mystical body of Christ.

I would certainly say the pope has done all that he can possibly do to fulfill Our Lady's request. I think it's very wrong to have any kind of suspicion or doubt about the Holy Father. It's very unworthy of true Catholics. As Director of the National Center, I receive many letters asking this question. I reply that the consecration of the world is wholly the business of the pope. My business as a Catholic is to live a life of personal consecration to the Blessed Mother and to help as many other individuals make and live that personal consecration to Our Lady. I am not responsible for the whole world or the whole Church—the pope is—and we must pray for him and help him through obedience, love and trust. It is very sad that people who claim to be devotees of the message of Fatima are so hypercritical of the pope and the bishops. Their attitude does a great deal to undermine the Fatima message. I hope that not even one person in the United States would belong to the Blue Army if he or she harbored an attitude of distrust and criticism toward the Holy Father or the bishops. We have to work with the bishops and the Holy Father. Sometimes we may not particularly like an individual, or may disagree with certain positions, but the bishops govern the Church in the name of Jesus. We have to work with them, respect them and love them.

I recall the moment when the bishop ordains a priest. The priest puts his hand in the bishop's hand, and the bishop looks him in the eye and says, "Do you promise me and my successor obedience and respect? Not only are priests expected to obey and respect the bishop, but so are all of the baptized.

So if you want to practice the message of Fatima, you must love the pope, trust him and the bishops and try to work in communion with the bishops.

As I mentioned in my talk, we get sidetracked on Fatima very easily. I think earlier a lot of people just concentrated on the "secret" and there was a lot of hype—during the 1950s, Fatima Countdown, for example. When is 1960 coming, as if the pope had to reveal the secret. The secret was given to him and he could reveal it if he thought it was wise. He had to make a judgment of prudence and Pope John XXIII, Paul VI, and John Paul II all made the decision not to reveal it to the Church. People said he won't tell us the secret so we are not going to follow Fatima anymore. As if that's all Fatima was! People today are holding on to the collegial consecration and making that the whole message. By expanding one small part, they are ignoring the mission of Our Lady, which is to make people holy.

Many priests hear Confessions at shrines. Priests ordained by Archbishop Lefebvre are in America and they hear Confessions. Are these Confessions valid ones? Do these priests have faculties to administer absolution?

Fr. Bertrand de Margerie:

That's a very complex issue because, first of all, there are priests who have been ordained by Archbishop Lefebvre and who have since been reconciled with the Holy See. So they can have faculties if they receive them from their bishop. As far as concerns the priests ordained by Archbishop Lefebvre, who have not been reconciled with the Holy See, they do not have the faculties because they are all suspended. They don't have the right to celebrate Mass or the sacraments. They are in the same position as Archbishop Lefebvre himself. It may be, nonetheless, that some of the faithful ignore the distinction between the Sacrament of Holy Orders and the giving of faculties.

What about the absolution of the Orthodox?

Fr. Bertrand de Margerie:

The absolution of the Orthodox differs because there is general agreement among Catholic theologians and in the Catholic Church that, by sort of indirect, implicit allowance of the Church, Orthodox priests can absolve the faithful of the Orthodox Church. This doesn't mean that Catholics can go and receive absolution from an Orthodox priest except, for instance, if the Catholic in question were traveling in Russia, and there were no Catholic priest available in that region, then according to the ecumenical directory of the Holy See, he could receive absolution from an Orthodox priest.

The Blessed Virgin was given the highest honor by God. Was the teaching of the council biased by ecumenism, which felt that we have to downplay Mary in order to win back our separated brethren?

Fr. Eamon R. Carroll:

No council in history ever said more about the Mother of Jesus than the Second Vatican Council. All the same, the council turned out be not the cause of but the occasion for a great explosion of unrest in the Church. Many of us will remember that on the eve of the council, which began in the fall of 1962, there was enormous optimism that the Church here in America was entering a new period of expansion. Many seminaries were enlarged and new ones were built. Religious houses were being built all over and it was thought there would be such a great growth in vocations that we would hardly be able to provide for all of them. What the council did was to provide the occasion for some deep unrest in the Church to rise to the surface. Prior to the council, even our Protestant brothers and sisters would have said that the most obvious mark of Roman Catholics was their devotion to the saints, especially to the Virgin Mary.

However, we might have remembered that after every council (this was true for example of the First Vatican Council a century ago) there has been a period of serious upset, sometimes very serious, and the upset in our Church has shown itself precisely in that area which was such a strongly identifying characteristic of our Catholic life—devotion to Our Lady.

Anyone who has taken the council documents seriously, as well as the interpretations of them that have been suggested by the popes and bishops since, recognize full well that there was no bending backwards to the council to try to come to terms with Protestant objections. There was a deliberate attempt indeed to be sensitive to Protestant difficulties and to find a common ground in which our Protestant brothers and sisters, at least in some degree, might join us in our veneration of Our Lady, but there was no attempt whatsoever, and the careful reading of the documents indicates this quite clearly, there was no attempt whatsoever to play down Our Lady's role. Quite the contrary! Her position in the council comes through more gloriously, more beautifully, more profoundly than ever before in any Church document. And it is only with the passage of years (we are twenty-five years after the council) that we are beginning to discover some of these riches and to come out of the woods, out of the forest of confusion and embarrassed silence about neglect of Our Lady in homilies and other forms of instruction. We realize how important she has always been to the Church, how important she remains and how as the Star of Evangelization, as the Holy Father called her, she is also a way to Christ. This is true also in some of the non-Catholic Christian world.

Regarding the secret that was given to the children of Fatima, is it true that Pope John XXIII read the secret and felt it was too frightening to tell the world?

Fr. Eamon R. Carroll:

From the accounts that I consulted, it seems that he read it and felt that it was too dreadful to reveal to the world. The most recent thing I looked at with respect to this was a book published a few years ago—a book by my friend Father Alonso, who died in 1980 and who had been commissioned to do the official history of Fatima in twenty-five volumes. He completed seventeen of the volumes before he died, and one of the few books of his that has been translated into English from Spanish concerns the secret of Fatima. He addresses the question of the secret and says that, as far as he was able to ascertain, there was absolutely no substance to the claim. It almost seems, from the way he writes, that at some stage in his investigation, he himself had been informed very closely about that secret. But even if he had not been, his knowledge of the circumstances and his friendship with Lucia and his intimate knowledge of the whole Fatima history, qualified him uniquely to talk about it. His point was that there is no *one* secret of Fatima. It is the total message, that is important, the message of prayer and penance. There is no new gospel that we are looking for. There is no forecast, no prophecy of imminent catastrophy, no more than any other authentic prophecy is an apocalyptic warning. However, the genuine prophecies do tend to warn us because we are a sinful people. We need to be reminded constantly of our need for prayer, penance, and reparation and turning back to the Lord.

I have heard that the basic elements of the message—prayer, sacrifice and devotion to the Immaculate Heart—are each fulfilled in the Mass. Can you explain?

Fr. Bertrand de Margerie:

The Mass itself is a prayer and all those who participate in the Mass are praying. The Mass is a sacrifice, the most supreme sacrifice, the sacrifice of the incarnate Son of God renewed among us. All those who participate in the Mass should, according to Pope Pius XII and to the Second Vatican Council, offer themselves as victims in union with Christ to the Father for the salvation of the world. Undoubtedly, the basic elements of prayer and sacrifice are contained in the Mass and fulfilled. Concerning devotion to the Immaculate Heart of Mary, I would say that in a very implicit way one might also hold this position in the sense that no Mass is ever celebrated without a mention of the name of Mary. However, there is a vast difference between what is implicit and what is explicit. It is obviously impossible to declare that, on an explicit level, devotion to the Immaculate Heart of Mary is contained in the Mass. But one might say that even if it is not explicit in the Mass, a certain attitude of love towards the Mother of God, who is also loving towards us, is indeed contained in the celebration of the Mass. That is why the organic union of churches in one unique, visible, universal Church will never be possible without recognition by the separated Christians of ecclesial communities of the very unique role of the Virgin Mary in the plan of salvation.

Why did the Church not wait until Lucia died to start the veneration of the other two seers?

Fr. Eamon R. Carroll:

I have no answer to that. The only possible answer that occurs to me is the same that would occur to all of you—the investigation was done with extreme care and the congregation being responsible for that, and ultimately the Holy Father, decided that indeed the virtues of these two holy children were heroic virtues and that the cause could proceed. Beyond that I cannot guess, and obviously there is a great confidence placed in Lucia, who is still alive (and now eighty-two to eighty-three years old). Beyond that, it is an unusual aspect and the question zeroes in on that aspect, as well.

Until the year 1960, Christian doctrine was taught in

parochial schools. How come so many graduates of these schools and even of Catholic universities left or became dissatisfied with the Church—priests, religious and lay people?

Fr. Eamon R. Carroll:

Again, none of us has an easy answer to that question. Sometimes there is a loss of faith, perhaps due to society, or some overall confusion in the Church, from which no one is immune. The priests and religious are human beings and they share the trials and temptations and unfortunately the doubts and affections of their lay brothers and lay sisters.

I would say as strongly as possible, however, that we should not neglect the great things the Holy Spirit has led the Church to do—a great broadening of lay participation in the work of the Church, an opening up of the liturgy in many respects, a greater social consciousness and certainly a recovering devotion to Our Lady on a very deep, biblical and traditional basis. These are things that the Holy Spirit has surely done through the council and since. We would be lacking in Christian joy if we neglected these great things. This calls for great patience in a time of darkness and suffering, but there is no cause for despair.

Is there a contradiction between how pained the Blessed Mother is over what happens among men and the belief of the eternal happiness we will achieve in heaven? How can we find happiness if the source of our happiness is weeping?

Fr. Eamon R. Carroll:

This again strikes me as an excellent example of the way God and his mercy, through the Mother of Jesus, accommodates Himself to our need. St. Paul tells us we are called to fill up what is wanting in the sufferings of Christ. We are the Church, the Church which as the Body of Christ continues to suffer in his members. The Risen Christ, the human Jesus, who is in the glory of the Father, is incapable of suffering as a human being, but he suffers still in his members. God in his mercy has permitted and willed that the Mother of Jesus should show herself weeping, as at La Salette, as Our Lady of Sorrows, at Fatima, and in other manifestations to indicate that the body of her Son, (we are the body of her Son) is still in this place of pilgrimage entering into the sufferings of the Lord.

One thing we must avoid, and it doesn't come through ever in any authentic appearance, is to think that justice belongs to the Risen Jesus and mercy belongs to his Mother. That's foolishness. We are accused of doing that, as Catholics, by those who do not understand us. It is thought that we regard Jesus as the severe and just judge and that we go to his Mother, because we can get around Him that way. That's a trap door approach to heaven—get to heaven and Peter turns us away, so we go to the back door and Our Lady lets us in. That's rotten catechesis. Even the smallest children should never be told this story because they may never outlive it. Our Lady's will of mercy is one with her Son. She has no other will than his will and God in his love has shown us his mercy through his Mother and continues to do so in her appearances in human history. So there is no question whatsoever of the Mother of Jesus being the refuge of sinners because she alone has mercy and justice, and justice alone is given over to her Son. Quite the contrary. Everything she has is his and as her will was one with his during her life on earth, ("Do whatever He tells you") it is impossible even more so now in the glory of heaven. So it's a very important consideration to realize when we hear of Mary appearing to our brothers and sisters there on pilgrimage with us and showing herself as deploring the sins of the world that we think it is very much in terms of our present need. She herself is in joy, but the Church, her Son's Church, her Son's body, of which she is the Mother, is still in suffering and is entering into the sufferings of her Son.

Is the book *True Devotion to Mary* the best way to study Our Lady and, if so, should it be promoted as a study book for all Marian groups as a special project?

Fr. Frederick L. Miller:

I certainly think that would be a good idea. Is it the best way to study Our Lady? As many of you know I am personally devoted to this and do a great deal to promote it. However, following the principles that Father Carroll spoke of, the Church leaves us free, even regarding the Rosary. What the Church really imposes on us is the Sunday Eucharist and the observance of the moral law. There is a great freedom in devotions, as long as our faith and our understanding of the moral law are intact. So I don't think we should say everyone has to practice True Devotion or make the consecration of St. Louis de Montfort, because the Church does not demand that. However, the Holy Father is very much taken with St. Louis de Montfort's way. Since young adulthood, he has practiced St. Louis' True Devotion and highly recommends it. He recommends it in *Redemptoris Mater*. So certainly one way to be in communion with him today, would be to understand and try to practice True Devotion.

If I remember well, in the book of St. Louis Marie Grignon de Montfort, he says himself that all are called to this True Devotion.

Fr. Frederick L. Miller:

Yes, to this form—everyone must have devotion to Our Lady but not necessarily in this way. I think it would be a good idea for groups, the cells of the World Apostolate of Fatima, to study True Devotion. We have been promoting this idea through videotapes, and articles in *SOUL*. I write an article on True Devotion to Our Lady for each issue. We have to be careful, though, not to impose things that the Church does not impose.

What connection can we draw between the prophecy of Don Bosco concerning the two pillars of victory, Jesus and the Eucharist and Mary, and the triumph of the Immaculate Heart of Mary, promised at Fatima?

Fr. Eamon R. Carroll:

I think we can draw an extremely close connection. There is a pattern running through the appearances of Our Lady and the lives of the saints within the last couple of centuries—I suppose one could extend that back to the time of Jesus Himself. Surely de Montfort's preaching in 1716, Don Bosco's in the last century and Our Lady's appearance at Fatima in the present century have a consistency of authenticity and I challenge none of them. To that degree they repeat the same message: the centrality of the Eucharist and the place of Our Lady in Catholic doctrine and Catholic devotion.

A Final Thought

I would like to thank Father Carroll for his splendid doctrinal presentation this morning. When you receive the tapes and the texts, I think you will possess a very important document for interpreting things and forming attitudes. I am sure that Father Carroll's talk will bear great fruit in the years ahead. We should reflect upon it and study it because its sound theology will help us base our devotion to Our Lady on the word of God and the teaching of the Church.

I would also like to thank Father de Margerie for his beautiful homily during the offering of the Mass, and I would like to connect Father de Margerie's and Father De Marchi's homily—a very touching reflection on the children of Fatima in this way: I have often felt that sometimes we who are involved with Marian movements can just isolate ourselves and see the movement as having to do only with prayer. Obviously prayer holds a primary place in our lives and we have to give, as Father De

Marchi said, an hour or two a day to prayer. It seems that when you give the time for prayer you have time for everything else and when you don't have time for prayer, you don't seem to have time for anything else either.

Prayer must have primacy in our lives, but sometimes Marian people think that the Christian life is simply that—saying the Rosary, having all night vigils and statue visitations. We forget that no one ever got into heaven for saying a Rosary. No one ever got into heaven for going to an all night vigil. These devotions help us and strengthen us to do God's will—and God's will is charity. We must love one another and love the poor, the oppressed, the sick, the dying and the minorities. Father de Margerie has encouraged us very beautifully today to put our love for Mary into practice—to love the poor, the oppressed, the minorities—specifically the Hispanics, whose population is rapidly increasing in the Church in America. In many ways, I believe the future of the Church in America will be with the minorities. If we ignore them, we will lose them as we have lost many already.

Father De Marchi told us that the children of Fatima, in that little hamlet, became missionaries, just as St. Thérèse shortly before became a missionary and patroness of the missions in a cloistered convent through prayer and sacrifice. We cannot simply look in our own back yards, in our own parish. We must look out into the world. We all have a responsibility for the salvation of the world. We must be missionaires through prayer, through charity, through sharing what we have with the poor. I hope one of the graces that comes through this symposium is that each of us becomes more deeply apostolic through the mediation of Our Blessed Mother.

God bless you!

Rev. Frederick L. Miller

CONTRIBUTORS

Rev. Robert I. Bradley, S.J. is a professor of theology and ecclesiastical history at the Notre Dame Catechetical Institute in Arlington, Va. and a visiting professor at Christendom College in Front Royal, Va. Father Bradley holds a doctorate in history from Columbia University and another in theology from the Angelicum in Rome. He is a contributor to the *New Catholic Encyclopedia* and various journals.

Rev. Eamon R. Carroll, O. Carm., is a professor of theology at Loyola University of Chicago. He served for twenty-five years on the theological faculty of the Catholic University of America (1957-80) and is past president of the Catholic Theological Society of America and The Mariological Society of America.

Rev. John De Marchi, I.M.C., is a missionary of the Consolata Society for Foreign Missions who operates a mission in Addis Ababa, Ethiopia, that includes schools, hospitals, an orphanage, a home for handicapped children and a leprosarium. Father De Marchi traveled to Fatima as a young priest in 1943 to study the event. His authoritative book, *Fatima, The Full Story*, is a result of his efforts and interviews with Sister Lucia and witnesses to the apparitions.

Rev. Frederick L. Miller is the Executive Director of the World Apostolate of Fatima National Center in Washington, N.J. A priest of the Archdiocese of Newark, he is an instructor for the Notre Dame Catechetical Institute in Arlington, Va. and a doctoral candidate at the Pontifical University of St. Thomas Aquinas in Rome. He is a great promoter of St. Louis de Montfort's True Devotion to Mary.

CONTRIBUTORS (cont.)

Rev. René Laurentin is a scripture scholar and professor of theology at the Catholic University of Angers, France. He was a peritus at the Second Vatican Council and is a pioneer of the methods of theological investigation approved by the council. His book, *La Question Mariale (Mary in the Church)* was a critical but constructive assessment of the Marian movement in the Church.

Rev. Bertrand de Margerie, S.J. of Paris is a member of the Pontifical Roman Academy of St. Thomas Aquinas. He is the author of some fifteen books including *Christ for the World* and *Christianity in History*. He has taught theology - specializing in the Heart of Jesus, Penance and the Eucharist - in the United States and in Latin America.

More Books and Tapes from the World Apostolate of Fatima

37362	**FATIMA IN LUCIA'S OWN WORDS** - This book of memoirs by Sr. Lucia is one of the outstanding works of modern Catholic literature of our time. 200 pp., paper.	$ 5.95
35529	**"THERE IS NOTHING MORE"** - The Rosary, scapular, Immaculate Heart and the Fatima Message. 368 pp., paper.	$ 5.95
38195	**BEHOLD YOUR MOTHER: American Bishops' Pastoral Letter** Concerns authentic Marian devotion. 66 pp., paper.	$ 3.75
38229	**CITY OF GOD** - Detailed life of the Blessed Virgin by Mary of Agreda. 4 volumes, 2676 pp., hardcover.	$49.00
38263	**CITY OF GOD (Abridged)** - Single volume abridgment of the City of God. 794 pp., paper.	$12.50
38344	**MARIAN REFLECTIONS** - The Angelus Messages of Pope John Paul II. Marian homilies from the Holy Year. 140 pp., paper.	$ 5.95
38350	**A HEART FOR ALL** - The Immaculate Heart of Mary in the message of Fatima. 207 pp., hardcover.	$ 3.95
38385	**MOTHER OF THE REDEEMER** - Encyclical letter of Pope John Paul II. Summarizes the Church's Marian teaching. 79 pp., paper.	$ 1.50
38390	**SERMONS OF ST. FRANCIS DE SALES ON OUR LADY** - Teachings on Mary from a saint and doctor of the Church. 219 pp., paper.	$ 8.00
38417	**THE GLORIES OF MARY** - by St. Alphonsus de Liguori. A glorious book about Mary. 670 pp., paper.	$ 5.00
38518	**TRUE DEVOTION TO MARY** - by St. Louis Grignion de Montfort. A classical masterpiece on true devotion, showing the need to go to Jesus through Mary. 85 pp., paper.	$ 4.50
38145	**FIRST LADY OF THE WORLD - A Popular History of Devotion to Mary** - by Peter Lappin. 192 pp., paper.	$ 9.95
38133	**DICTIONARY OF MARY** - Sets forth the most important Catholic teachings about Mary in dictionary form. 416 pp., paper.	$ 6.00
37447	**FATIMA: THE GREAT SIGN** - by Francis Johnston. The role of Fatima in the Church. 152 pp., paper.	$ 4.95
37549	**MEET THE WITNESSES** - by John M. Haffert. Interviews with witnesses of the miracle of the sun. 160 pp., illustrated, paper.	$ 3.25
37583	**OUR LADY OF FATIMA** - by William T. Walsh. A classic account of the apparitions. 223 pp., paper.	$ 4.95
49703	**"AND FROM THAT HOUR..."** - Pope John Paul II's historic homily at Fatima, May 13, 1982.	$ .50

49716	**THE SIGNIFICANCE OF MARY FOR WOMEN** - by Dr. Joyce A. Little..	$ .50
40983	**17 PAPAL DOCUMENTS ON THE ROSARY** - Contains *Marialis Cultis*. Superb reference. 150 pp., paper........................	$ 2.00
51313	**BROWN SCAPULAR OF MOUNT CARMEL** - by Fr. Barry Bossa, S.A.C. Illustrated history. 50 pp., paper........................	$ 2.50

Audio Tapes

361564	**Mary in the Scriptures** by Msgr. James C. Turro....................	$ 3.95
361569	**True Devotion to Mary** by Sr. Mary Frederick, M.C.................	$ 3.95
362147	**Fifteen decades of the Rosary** and Rosary history................	$10.95
361915	**The First National Fatima Symposium.** Study the message of Fatima in-depth. Hear all the presentations in this six cassette album...	$24.00
362745	**Mother Teresa** speaks to pilgrims at the Blue Army Shrine of the Immaculate Heart of Mary. Fr. Frederick Miller addresses Total Consecration to Jesus through Mary (side 2)......................	$ 4.95

NAME _____

STREET _____

CITY _____

STATE _____ ZIP _____

**World Apostolate
of Fatima
(The Blue Army, USA)**
Mountain View Road
P.O. Box 976
Washington, NJ 07882
(908) 689-1700

Qty.	Item #	Color/Description	Price Each	Total Price

Please add proper shipping and handling charge shown below

Value of Order	USA	Foreign
$0 - $1.99	$ 1.05	
$2.00 - $24.99	$ 3.45	Customers
$25.00 - $49.99	$ 5.25	will be billed
$50.00 - $100.00	$ 7.55	for postage.
Over $100	Add 15%	

Subtotal
N.J. residents:
Add 7% sales tax
Shipping & Handling
Donation
Total*

Please make checks payable to: **World Apostolate of Fatima**
* U.S. funds payable through a U.S. bank. Postal money orders in U.S. funds are accepted.
Prices subject to change without notice

Exploring Fatima